Intensive Practice 4B
Preface

Singapore Math® Intensive Practice is a series of 12 books written to provide challenging supplementary material for Singapore math programs.

The primary objective of this series of books is to help students generate greater interest in mathematics and gain more confidence in solving mathematical problems. To achieve this, special features are incorporated in the series.

SPECIAL FEATURES

Topical Review

Enables students of mixed abilities to be exposed to a good variety of questions which are of varying levels of difficulty so as to help them develop a better understanding of mathematical concepts and their applications.

Mid-Year or End-Of-Year Review

Provides students with a good review that summarizes the topics learned in Singapore math programs.

Take the Challenge!

Deepens students' mathematical concepts and helps develop their mathematical reasoning and higher-order thinking skills as they practice their problem-solving strategies.

More Challenging Problems

Stimulate students' interest through challenging and thought-provoking problems which encourage them to think critically and creatively as they apply their knowledge and experience in solving these problems.

Why this Series?

Students will find this series of books a good complement and supplement to Singapore math programs. The comprehensive coverage certainly makes this series a valuable resource for teachers, parents and tutors.

It is hoped that the special features in this series of books will inspire and spur young people to achieve better mathematical competency and greater mathematics problem-solving skills.

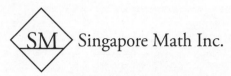
Singapore Math Inc.

Copyright © 2004 Singapore Math Inc.

Published by
Singapore Math Inc.
19535 SW 129th Ave.
Tualatin, OR 97062
U.S.A.
E-mail: customerservice@singaporemath.com
www.singaporemath.com

First published 2004
Reprinted 2005, 2007, 2008, 2009, 2010, 2012, 2013,
2014, 2016, 2018, 2019, 2020

Singapore Math® Intensive Practice 4B
ISBN 978-1-932906-07-3

Printed in China

Our special thanks to Jenny Kempe for her assistance in editing
Singapore Math® Intensive Practice.

Intensive Practice 4B
Contents

Topic 1: Decimals

What is a **Decimal**?
A decimal is a fraction, expressed as equal parts of 10's, 100's or 1000's with a decimal point.

Example 1:

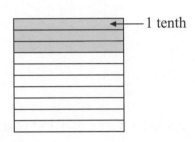

1 tenth

The diagram above shows 3 out of 10 equal parts in 1 whole.

Written as a fraction, it is $\frac{3}{10}$.

Written as a decimal, it is 0 . 3

decimal point ——┘ └—— 3 tenths

The digit '3' is in the tenths place or the **1st decimal place**.

Example 2:

Each tenth of the whole is now divided into 10 smaller equal parts.

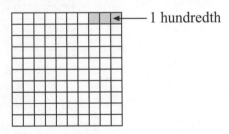

1 hundredth

The diagram above shows 3 out of 100 equal parts in 1 whole.

Written as a fraction, it is $\frac{3}{100}$.

Written as a decimal, it is 0 . 0 3

decimal point ——┘ └—— 3 hundredths

The digit '3' is in the hundredths place or the **2nd decimal place**.

1

Example 3:

Each hundredth of the whole is now further divided into 10 smaller equal parts.

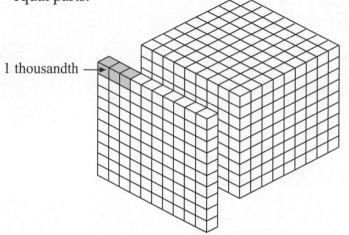

1 thousandth

The diagram above shows 3 out of 1000 equal parts in 1 whole.

Written as a fraction, it is $\dfrac{3}{1000}$.

Written as a decimal, it is 0 . 0 0 3

decimal point ———↑   ↑——— 3 thousandths

The digit '3' is in the thousandths place or the **3rd decimal place**.

Example 4:

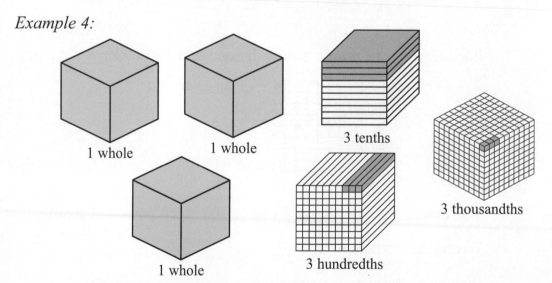

1 whole   1 whole   3 tenths

1 whole   3 hundredths   3 thousandths

When a number, as shown above, does not make up a whole number, it can be expressed as a fraction or a decimal.

Written as a fraction, it is $3 + \dfrac{3}{10} + \dfrac{3}{100} + \dfrac{3}{1000}$

$$= 3 + \dfrac{300}{1000} + \dfrac{30}{1000} + \dfrac{3}{1000}$$

$$= 3\dfrac{333}{1000}$$

Written as a decimal, it is 3.333

1. Complete the table below.

Dollar bill	Number of $1 bills	Fraction of a $1000-bill		
		Decimal fraction	Fraction	Decimal
Five hundred	500	$\dfrac{500}{1000}$ or $\dfrac{50}{100}$ or $\dfrac{5}{10}$	$\dfrac{1}{2}$	0.5
One hundred	100			
Fifty	50			
Ten	10			
Five	5			
One	1			

2. Write the decimal in each box.

	Decimal	Thousands	Hundreds	Tens	Ones	Tenths	Hundredths	Thousandths
	99.9	—	—	9	9	9	—	—
(a)		—	1	2	3	4	5	—
(b)		—	7	0	7	0	7	—
(c)		6	3	8	0	0	8	3
(d)		—	—	8	2	3	0	4
(e)		7	0	4	5	0	0	9

3. For each question, fill in the box to complete the fraction and write the corresponding decimal in the blank.

(a) 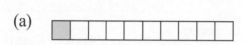 $\dfrac{1}{10}$ = _____

(b) 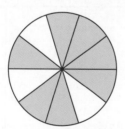 $\dfrac{5}{\boxed{}}$ = _____

(c) 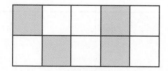 $\dfrac{\boxed{}}{10}$ = _____

(d) 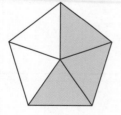 $\dfrac{7}{\boxed{}}$ = _____

(e) $\dfrac{\boxed{}}{5} = \dfrac{\boxed{}}{10}$ = _____

4

4. Write a decimal for each of the following.

(a) 2 tenths =   (b) 8 tenths =

(c) 10 tenths =   (d) 16 tenths =

(e) 2 ones 6 tenths =   (f) 16 ones 9 tenths =

5. Fill in the blanks. (1 whole = 10 tenths)

(a) 50 = _____ tenths   (b) 0.1 = _____ tenths

(c) 10 = _____ tenths   (d) 3.4 = _____ tenths

(e) 12.6 = _____ tenths (f) 7.5 = _____ tenths

6. Fill in the blanks.

(a) The numeral 67.3 is made up of 6 tens, 7 ones and _____ tenths.

(b) In 98.3, the digit '3' is in the _____ place.

(c) The value of the digit '9' in 7.9 is _____.

(d) In the numeral 40.6, the digit '4' stands for _____.

(e) 37.5 is 3 tens, 6 ones and _____ tenths.

(f) 6 ones, 2 tens and 8 tenths written as a decimal is _____.

(g) 8 ones and 24 tenths is the same as 10 ones and _____ tenths.

(h) 52 tenths is the same as 4 ones and _____ tenths.

7. Express each fraction as a decimal.
    (Change the fraction to an equivalent fraction with a denominator of 10 if necessary before expressing it as a decimal.)

(a) $\dfrac{9}{10}$ =   (b) $\dfrac{3}{10}$ =

(c) $1\dfrac{4}{10}$ =   (d) $4\dfrac{1}{5}$ =

(e) $8\dfrac{1}{2}$ =   (f) $10\dfrac{3}{5}$ =

5

8. Read the value indicated on the scale and give your answer as a decimal.

(a)

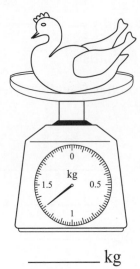

_____ kg

(b)

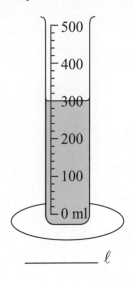

_____ ℓ

(c)

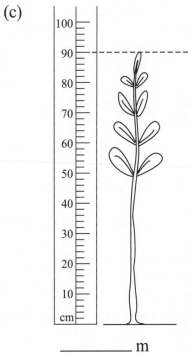

_____ m

(d)

_____ minutes

9. Express each decimal as a fraction in its simplest form.

(a) 0.7 =

(b) 1.2 =

(c) 4.4 =

(d) 7.8 =

(e) 13.6 =

(f) 20.9 =

10. Circle the smallest number in each set of decimals.

    (a)   3.4, 8.1, 2.9, 6.7   (b)   2.6, 1.9, 4.2, 0.8

    (c)   5.5, 6.4, 7.3, 8.2   (d)   11.2, 7.9, 5.3, 8

    (e)   16.9, 120.2, 19.7, 12.8   (f)   21.3, 24.9, 101.1, 13.7

11. Fill in the missing decimal in each box.

    (a)   Each equal unit on the number line stands for 0.1.

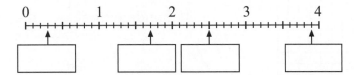

    (b)   Each equal unit on the number line stands for _____.

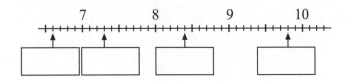

    (c)   Each equal unit on the number line stands for _____.

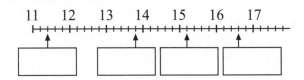

    (d)   Each equal unit on the number line stands for _____.

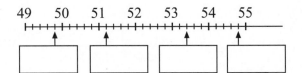

7

12. For each question, shade the diagram to show the given value. Fill in the box to complete the fraction and write the decimal in the blank.

(a)

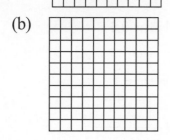

14 hundredths = $\dfrac{\boxed{}}{100}$ = _____

(b)

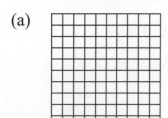

45 hundredths = $\dfrac{\boxed{}}{100}$ = _____

(c)

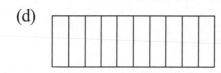

3 tenths = _____ hundredths

$= \dfrac{\boxed{}}{100}$ = _____

(d)

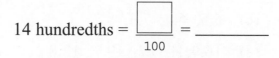

4 tenths = _____ hundredths

$= \dfrac{\boxed{}}{100}$ = _____

(e)

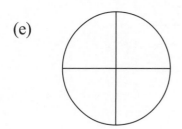

$\dfrac{1}{4} = \dfrac{\boxed{}}{100}$ = _____ hundredths

$=$ _____

(f)

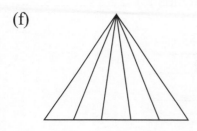

$\dfrac{3}{5} = \dfrac{\boxed{}}{100}$ = _____ hundredths

$=$ _____

13. Write a decimal for each of the following.

    (a) 2 hundredths =   (b) 18 hundredths =

    (c) 100 hundredths =   (d) 493 hundredths =

    (e) 37 hundredths =   (f) 173 hundredths =

14. Write a decimal for each of the following.

    (a) 3 tens, 2 ones, 4 tenths and 6 hundredths =

    (b) 10 tens, 3 ones, 9 tenths and 6 hundredths =

    (c) 7 tens, 22 tenths and 2 hundredths =

    (d) 6 hundreds, 7 ones, 35 tenths and 43 hundredths =

15. Fill in the blanks.
    (1 whole = 10 tenths = 100 hundredths; 1 tenth = 10 hundredths)

    (a) 80 = _____ tens   (b) 8 = _____ tenths

    (c) 0.8 = _____ tenths   (d) 0.88 = _____ hundredths

    (e) 1.8 = _____ hundredths

    (f) 18 tenths = _____ hundredths

16. Fill in the blanks.

    (a) In 95.12, the digit '2' is in the _____ place.

    (b) In 129.73, the digit '_____' is in the hundredths place.

    (c) The value of the digit '4' in 418.29 is _____.

    (d) The digit '5' in 98.75 stands for _____.

    (e) In 985.65, the value of the digit '5' in the ones place is _____ times the value of the same digit in the hundredths place.

    (f) The digit '3' has a value of _____ less than the value of the digit '2' in 111.23.

17. Express each fraction as a decimal.
(Change the fraction to an equivalent fraction with a denominator of 100 if necessary before expressing it as a decimal.)

(a) $\dfrac{9}{100} =$

(b) $\dfrac{75}{100} =$

(c) $1\dfrac{1}{4} =$

(d) $4\dfrac{8}{50} =$

(e) $7\dfrac{17}{20} =$

(f) $10\dfrac{11}{25} =$

18. Express each decimal as a fraction in its simplest form.

(a) $0.08 =$

(b) $0.23 =$

(c) $0.60 =$

(d) $1.86 =$

(e) $3.75 =$

(f) $26.05 =$

19. Circle the largest number in each set of decimals.

(a) 0.09, 1.83, 6.06, 0.94

(b) 4.38, 14.12, 8.23, 18.19

(c) 7.8, 0.81, 4, 9.04

(d) 8.03, 19.46, 20.1, 0.74

(e) 46.09, 100.2, 100.17, 92.8

(f) 31.6, 74.12, 101.15, 103.7

20. Fill in the missing decimal in each box.

(a) Each equal unit on the number line stands for 0.01.

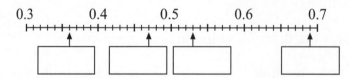

(b) Each equal unit on the number line stands for _____.

6.3   6.4   6.5   6.6

(c) Each equal unit on the number line stands for _____.

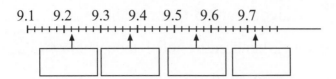

(d) Each equal unit on the number line stands for _____.

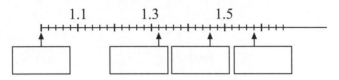

21. Fill in the missing fraction in each box.

(a) $1.66 = 1 + \dfrac{6}{10} + \boxed{}$

(b) $2.25 = 2 + \dfrac{2}{10} + \boxed{}$

(c) $6.78 = 6 + \boxed{} + \dfrac{8}{100}$

(d) $16.14 = 15 + \boxed{} + \dfrac{4}{100}$

22. Write each value as a decimal.

(a) $8 + \dfrac{1}{10} + \dfrac{7}{100} =$ _____

(b) $12 + \dfrac{5}{100} =$ _____

(c) _____ $= 17 + \dfrac{1}{2} + \dfrac{16}{100}$

(d) _____ $= 90 + \dfrac{16}{10}$

23. Write a decimal for each of the following.

(a) 5 thousandths = _____

(b) 375 thousandths = _____

(c) 40 thousandths = _____

(d) 108 thousandths = _____

(e) 1234 thousandths = _____

(f) 3145 thousandths = _____

11

24. Write a decimal for each of the following.

    (a) 2 tenths, 5 hundredths and 5 thousandths = _____

    (b) 1 one, 5 tenths, 2 hundredths and 1 thousandth = _____

    (c) 12 ones and 52 thousandths = _____

    (d) 4 tens, 11 hundredths and 9 thousandths = _____

25. Fill in the blanks.

    (a) In 9.102, the digit '2' is in the _____ place.

    (b) In 20.736, the digit '_____' is in the thousandths place.

    (c) The value of the digit '4' in 4001.321 is _____.

    (d) The digit '7' in 48.417 stands for _____.

    (e) In 0.565, the value of the digit '5' in the tenths place is _____ times the value of the same digit in the thousandths place.

    (f) The digit '3' has a value _____ less than the value of the digit '2' in 2.003.

26. Express each fraction as a decimal.
(Change the fraction to an equivalent fraction with a denominator of 1000 if necessary before expressing it as a decimal.)

    (a) $\dfrac{106}{1000} =$ (b) $\dfrac{80}{1000} =$

    (c) $1\dfrac{9}{200} =$ (d) $5\dfrac{475}{500} =$

    (e) $29\dfrac{104}{250} =$ (f) $14\dfrac{1}{8} =$

27. Express each decimal as a fraction in its simplest form.

    (a) 0.006 =   (b) 0.075 =

    (c) 0.555 =   (d) 1.020 =

    (e) 7.375 =   (f) 2.480 =

28. Arrange the numbers in ascending order.

   (a)   0.023, 0.203, 2.003, 0.302

   _____

   (b)   3.108, 1.083, 1.38, 3.018

   _____

   (c) $2\frac{1}{5}$, 1.005, $\frac{21}{20}$, 2.5

   _____

   (d)   4.951, $3\frac{6}{10}$, $4\frac{7}{8}$, $3\frac{106}{1000}$

   _____

29. Arrange the numbers in descending order.

   (a)   3.8, 8.382, 0.832, 2.083

   _____

   (b)   9.089, 9.908, 89.09, 10.809

   _____

   (c)   0.742, $1\frac{1}{2}$, 1.555, $\frac{23}{10}$

   _____

   (d)   2.109, $1\frac{9}{10}$, 20.19, $2\frac{19}{100}$

   _____

30. Fill in the missing decimal in each box.

(a) Each equal unit on the number line stands for 0.001.

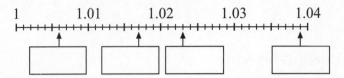

(b) Each equal unit on the number line stands for _____ .

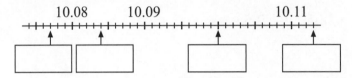

(c) Each equal unit on the number line stands for _____ .

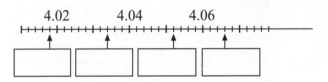

(d) Each equal unit on the number line stands for _____ .

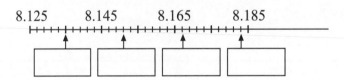

31. Fill in the missing fraction in each box.

(a) $2.287 = 2 + \dfrac{2}{10} + \boxed{} + \dfrac{7}{1000}$

(b) $5.059 = 5 + \boxed{}$

(c) $21.379 = 21 + \dfrac{37}{100} + \boxed{}$

(d) $10.943 = 9 + \boxed{} + \dfrac{43}{1000}$

32. Write each value as a decimal.

(a) $3 + \dfrac{3}{10} + \dfrac{37}{100} = $ _____

(b) $10 + \dfrac{9}{20} = $ _____

(c) _____ $= 15 + \dfrac{1}{4} + \dfrac{36}{1000}$

(d) _____ $= 80 + \dfrac{156}{100} + \dfrac{1}{1000}$

33. Round each of the following to the nearest whole number.

Example:

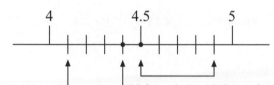

Values 0.5 to 0.9 can be approximated to the value of 1.
Hence, 4.5 is 5 when rounded to the nearest whole number.

Values below 0.5, that is 0.1 to 0.4, are too small to be approximated to the value of 1.
Hence, 4.4 is 4 when rounded to the nearest whole number.

(a) $4.7 \approx$ _____

(b) $0.41 \approx$ _____

(c) $\$9.59 \approx \$$_____

(d) $\$38.45 \approx \$$_____

(e) $2.847 \approx$ _____

(f) 15.358 km $\approx$ _____ km

34. Round each of the following to 1 decimal place (or to the nearest tenth).

Example:

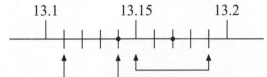

Values 0.05 to 0.09 can be approximated to the value of 0.1.
Hence, 13.17 is 13.2 when rounded to 1 decimal place.

Values below 0.05, that is 0.01 to 0.04, are too small to be approximated to the value of 0.1.
Hence, 13.14 is 13.1 when rounded to 1 decimal place.

(a) 0.93 ≈ _____   (b) 4.64 ≈ _____

(c) 10.35 m ≈ _____ m   (d) 27.05 kg ≈ _____ kg

(e) 6.783 km ≈ _____ km (f) 0.275 ℓ ≈ _____ ℓ

(g) 56.705 ≈ _____   (h) 23.018 ≈ _____

35. Round each of the following to 2 decimal places (or to the nearest hundredth).

Example

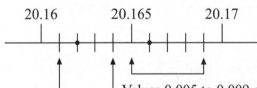

Values 0.005 to 0.009 can be approximated to the value of 0.01.
Hence, 20.166 is 20.17 when rounded to 2 decimal places.

Values below 0.005, that is 0.001 to 0.004, are too small to be approximated to the value of 0.01.
Hence, 20.162 is 20.16 when rounded to 2 decimal places.

(a) 0.256 ≈ _____   (b) 0.572 ≈ _____

(c) 1.083 kg ≈ _____ kg (d) 34.698 m² ≈ _____ m²

16

(e) 29.271 $\ell \approx$ _____ ℓ (f) 99.899 km $\approx$ _____ km

(g) 1.004 $\approx$ _____   (h) 1.995 $\approx$ _____

36. Write down the set of decimals that can be rounded to the given whole number.

    Example:

        9 : {8.5, 8.6, 8.7, 8.8, 8.9, 9.0, 9.1, 9.2, 9.3, 9.4}

    (a) 4 : {   }

    (b) 10 : {   }

    (c) 125 : {   }

37. Write down the set of decimals that can be rounded to the given number.

    Example:

        0.4 : {0.35, 0.36, 0.37, 0.38, 0.39, 0.40, 0.41, 0.42, 0.43, 0.44}

    (a) 0.9 : {   }

    (b) 13.8 : {   }

    (c) 200.0 : {   }

38. Write down the set of decimals that can be rounded to the given number.

    Example:

        0.30 : {0.295, 0.296, 0.297, 0.298, 0.299, 0.300, 0.301, 0.302, 0.303, 0.304}

    (a) 0.57 : {   }

    (b) 8.35 : {   }

    (c) 12.20 : {   }

39. Answer the following questions.

   (a) Clarissa weighs 70.5 lb.
       How much does she weigh, when rounded to the nearest pound?

   (b) A tree in a park is 20.48 yd tall.
       What is the height of the tree when rounded to the nearest yard?

   (c) After her shopping, Mrs. Kelly found that she had only $24.55 left.
       How much money did she have left, when rounded to the nearest dollar?

   (d) The distance between two cities is 299.512 km.
       How far apart are the two cities, when rounded to the nearest kilometer?

40. Circle all the possible actual values in each of the following.

   (a) Adrian has $10.50 when rounded to the nearest ten cents.
       The actual amount of money he has can be

       $10.45 $10.52 $10.55 $10.49 $10.40

(b)   The height of an apartment builiding is 78.0 m when rounded to 1 decimal place. The height of the apartment builidng can be

78.04 m   77.95 m   78.85 m   77.973 m   78.08 m

(c)   The volume of water in a tank is 25 gallons when rounded to the nearest gallon. The volume of water in the tank can be

25.9 gal   24.95 gal   25.609 gal   24.75 gal   25.045 gal

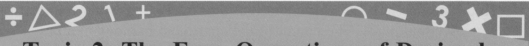
1. The purse contains some dollar bills and coins.

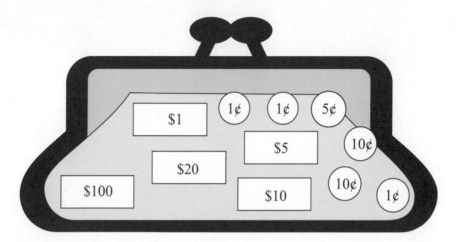

The total amount of money in the purse can be expressed as a decimal as shown below.

	Hundreds	Tens	Ones	Tenths	Hundredths
$100 – 1 hundred = 100	1				
$20 – 2 tens = 20		2			
$10 – 1 ten = 10		1			
$5 – 5 ones = 5			5		
$1 – 1 one = 1			1		
20¢ – 2 tenths = 0.2				2	
5¢ – 5 hundredths = 0.05					5
3¢ – 3 hundredths = 0.03					3
Total amount of money in dollars	**1**	**3**	**6**	**2**	**8**

decimal point

You may use the concept linking decimals and money to do the following.

Example 1:   0.3 + 0.2 → 30¢ + 20¢ = 50¢
                       → 0.5

Example 2: $0.07 + 0.16 \rightarrow 7¢ + 16¢ = 23¢$

$$\rightarrow 0.23$$

(a) $0.8 + 0.03 =$ _____

(b) $0.09 + 0.08 =$ _____

(c) $0.6 + 0.75 =$ _____

(d) $0.4 + 0.76 =$ _____

(e) $7 + 0.03 =$ _____

(f) $0.63 + 0.8 =$ _____

(g) $1.3 + 0.6 =$ _____

(h) $0.97 + 0.3 =$ _____

2. Add.

(a) $0.64 + 0.75 =$ _____

$$\begin{array}{r} 0.\,6\,4 \\ +\quad 0.\,7\,5 \\ \hline \\ \hline \end{array}$$

(b) $0.93 + 0.69 =$ _____

$$\begin{array}{r} 0.\,9\,3 \\ +\quad 0.\,6\,9 \\ \hline \\ \hline \end{array}$$

(c) $4 + 2.89 =$ _____

(d) $2.46 + 0.7 =$ _____

(e) $5.3 + 8.03 =$ _____

(f) $3.47 + 1.6 =$ _____

(g) $13.26 + 9.7 =$ _____

(h) $43.57 + 16.06 =$ _____

(i) $9.63 + 22.79 =$ _____

(j) $11.35 + 59.99 =$ _____

3. Estimate the answer by rounding each decimal to the nearest whole number.

(a) $3.8 + 7.29 \approx 4 + 7$

$$= \underline{\hspace{2cm}}$$

(b) $3.16 + 8.6 \approx$

$$= \underline{\hspace{2cm}}$$

(c) $5.18 + 2.03 \approx$

$$= \underline{\hspace{2cm}}$$

(d) $9.96 + 4.27 \approx$

$$= \underline{\hspace{2cm}}$$

(e) $26.7 + 1.49 \approx$

$$= \underline{\hspace{2cm}}$$

(f) $13.17 + 47.86 \approx$

$$= \underline{\hspace{2cm}}$$

4. Subtract.

(a)   0.09 – 0.05 = _____

(b)   0.86 – 0.25 = _____

(c)   1.48 – 0.27 = _____

(d)   1.5 – 0.56 = _____

$$\begin{array}{r} 1.\,4\,8 \\ -\quad 0.\,2\,7 \\ \hline \\ \hline \end{array}$$

$$\begin{array}{r} 1.\,5\,0 \\ -\quad 0.\,5\,6 \\ \hline \\ \hline \end{array}$$

(e)   8 – 4.03 = _____

(f)   4.9 – 2.37 = _____

(g)   19.06 – 5.7 = _____

(h)   23.7 – 6.81 = _____

(i)   39.72 – 7.04 = _____

(j)   14 – 9.54 = _____

5. Estimate the answer by rounding each decimal to the nearest whole number.

(a)   6.3 – 1.28 ≈ 6 – 1

  = _____

(b)   9.11 – 3.1 ≈

  = _____

(c)   11.0 – 4.8 ≈

  = _____

(d)   4.96 – 0.79 ≈

  = _____

(e)   26.39 – 14.6 ≈

  = _____

(f)   17.4 – 8.93 ≈

  = _____

6. Do the following. You may use the method shown in the example.

Example: 2.45 + 1.95 = 2.45 + 2 – 0.05
                    = 4.45 – 0.05
                    = 4.4

(a)   15.80 + 5.97 = 15.80 + _____ – _____

  = _____

(b) $21.68 + 10.99 = 21.68 + $ _____ $-$ _____

   $= $ _____

(c) $4.12 - 0.98 = 4.12 - 1 + 0.02$

   $= $ _____

(d) $10.69 - 6.96 = 10.69 - $ _____ $+$ _____

   $= $ _____

(e) $32.53 - 13.99 = 32.53 - $ _____ $+$ _____

   $= $ _____

7. Complete these magic squares so that the decimals in every row, column and diagonal have the same sum.

(a)

row →   ＼ diagonal   (b)

0.7		
	0.6	
0.9		0.5

↓ column

1.5	1.25	2.5
	1.75	

(c)

		0.85
	0.55	
0.25	0.95	

(d)

	0.7	
	0.9	1.5
	1.1	

8. Do the following.

(a)   Add 18 tenths to 0.98.

(b) Find the difference between 9.85 and 24 hundredths.

(c) Round the sum of 4.76, 67.9 and 99.09 to 1 decimal place.

(d) A number is 13.2. A second number is 2.84 less. What is the second number?

(e) What is 64 tenths less than 16.48?

(f) After buying a shirt and a pair of jeans for a total of $61.45, Samuel had $13.25 left. How much did he have at first?

(g) A worker has 15 m of rope. He cuts it into 2 pieces of lengths 1.5 m and 4.75 m. What is the length of rope left?

(h) Mrs. Lee has $1\frac{3}{4}$ quarts of pineapple juice and 1.56 quarts of orange juice. What is the total amount of fruit juice when she mixes them together?

(i)   Gerald clocked 10.18 seconds while Mark managed to finish 0.2 seconds faster than Gerald in a 100-meter race. How long did Mark take to complete the race?

(j)   Tim took 0.4 hour to finish his dinner. Sam started his dinner 0.25 hour after Tim had started his dinner and took 0.7 hour to finish it. How much longer did Sam take to finish his dinner after Tim had finished his?

9. Multiply.

(a) $0.03 \times 4 = 3$ hundredths $\times 4$
      $= 12$ hundredths

      $=$ _____

(b) $0.9 \times 4 = 9$ tenths $\times 4$
      $= 36$ tenths

      $=$ _____

(c) $0.9 \times 6 =$ _____

(d) $0.06 \times 8 =$ _____

(e) $0.13 \times 3 =$ _____

(f) $3.48 \times 7 =$ _____

$$\begin{array}{r} 0.\,1\,3 \\ \times \qquad 3 \\ \hline \\ \hline \end{array}$$

$$\begin{array}{r} 3.\,4\,8 \\ \times \qquad 7 \\ \hline \\ \hline \end{array}$$

(g) $\$0.68 \times 5 = \$$_____

(h) $\$8.06 \times 2 = \$$_____

(i) $11.24 \times 6 =$ _____

(j) $9 \times 38.75 =$ _____

(k) $308.4 \times 3 =$ _____

(l) $104.9 \times 7 =$ _____

10. For each of the following, estimate the product by rounding the decimal to the nearest whole number.

(a) $7.2 \times 6 \approx 7 \times 6$

= _____

(b) $14.85 \times 7 \approx$

= _____

(c) $16.8 \times 3 \approx$

= _____

(d) $5 \times 33.5 \approx$

= _____

(e) $\$42.06 \times 9 \approx$

= _____

(f) $3 \times \$84.92 \approx$

= _____

11. Divide.

(a) $0.9 \div 3 = 9$ tenths $\div 3$
            $= 3$ tenths

= _____

(b) $0.42 \div 6 = 42$ hundredths $\div 6$
            $= 7$ hundredths

= _____

(c) $8.1 \div 9 =$ _____

(d) $5.6 \div 7 =$ _____

(e) $0.7 \div 2 =$ _____

(f) $2.3 \div 5 =$ _____

$$\begin{array}{r} 0.3 \\ 2\overline{)0.70} \\ -\ 0 \\ \hline 7 \\ -\ 6 \\ \hline 1\ 0 \end{array}$$

$$5\overline{)2.3}$$

(g) $\$1 \div 4 = \$$_____

(h) $\$30 \div 8 = \$$_____

$$4\overline{)\$1.0}$$

$$8\overline{)\$30}$$

(i) $15.18 \div 6 =$ _____ (j) $14.04 \div 4 =$ _____

(k) $65.2 \div 5 =$ _____ (l) $92.33 \div 7 =$ _____

12. Find the value of each of the following and then round your answer to the nearest whole number and to 1 decimal place.

		Round to the nearest whole number	Round to 1 decimal place
(a)	9.3×3		
(b)	4.21×6		
(c)	$8.1 \div 9$		
(d)	$57.75 \div 7$		
(e)	$7 \div 2$		
(f)	2.3×5		
(g)	$12.2 \div 4$		
(h)	$30 \div 8$		
(i)	15.78×6		
(j)	14.44×4		
(k)	$65.2 \div 5$		
(l)	39.22×7		

13. Divide and round your answer to 2 decimal places.

Example: $1 \div 3 \approx$ **0.33** (to 2 decimal places)

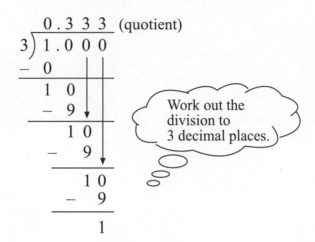

You will notice that the division shown above will continue in the same manner. The quotient is a recurring decimal. Where a fraction expressed as a decimal results in a recurring decimal or a decimal that has many decimal places, we may give the answer to a specified degree of accuracy of 1 or 2 decimal places.

(a) $3.59 \div 6 \approx$ _____   (b) $22 \div 7 \approx$ _____

(c) $16.58 \div 9 \approx$ _____   (d) $47.81 \div 8 \approx$ _____

14. For each of the following, estimate the quotient by rounding the decimal to the nearest whole number which can be divided by the given number without any remainder.

(a) $5.2 \div 3 \approx 6 \div 3$ (b) $1.12 \div 5 \approx 1 \div 5$

        $=$ _____ $=$ _____

(c) $26.7 \div 7 \approx$

   = _____

(d) $34.8 \div 8 \approx$

   = _____

(e) $71.08 \div 9 \approx$

   = _____

(f) $236.49 \div 4 \approx$

   = _____

15. Work out the following.

   (a) What are the two numbers if the sum of the two numbers is 5.2 and their difference is 0.4?

   (b) What are the two numbers if the sum of the two numbers is 7.5 and their difference is 1?

   (c) What are the two numbers if the sum of the two numbers is 6.5 and their product is 9?

   (d) What are the two numbers if the sum of the two numbers is 6.5 and their product is 0.64?

   (e) Estimate the value of 56.71×23.17. (Round each decimal to the nearest whole number.)

(f)   Mrs. White has 5.8 kg of sugar and Mrs. Gray has 9.5 kg of sugar. How much sugar must Mrs. Gray give to Mrs. White so that each of them will have the same amount of sugar?

(g)   A tailor used 3.6 m of cloth to sew a pair of long pants and $1\frac{1}{8}$ m of cloth to sew a shirt. How much cloth did he use to sew the two items?

(h)   Find the area and perimeter of a rectangle 17.8 cm long and 9 cm wide.

(i)   Dolly filled 3 jugs with equal amount of water. The total amount of water in the 3 jugs is 13.2 liters. How much water do 5 such jugs hold?

(j)   Frances went to the market with $31.90. She bought 5 lb of fish and had $10.40 left. What was the cost of each pound of fish?

(k)   A string 15 feet long is cut into 9 pieces of equal length. What is the length of each piece? Give your answer to 2 decimal places.

WORD PROBLEMS

1. Wendy's mother gave her $15 for an outing with her friends. She spent $1.05 on bus fare, $3.50 on lunch and 80 cents on a drink on her way home. How much did she have left?

2. There were 14.83 gallons of water in a tank at first. I discovered that 2.85 gallons of water leaked out from the bottom of the tank, so I added another 9.76 gallons of water. How much water is there in the tank now? Give the answer correct to 1 decimal place.

3. Terry took part in a triathlon in which he cycled, jogged and then swam. He cycled twice as far as he jogged and he jogged twice as far as he swam. If he jogged 20.7 km, what was the total distance he covered in all the three events? Round the answer to the nearest kilometer.

4. Andrea bought a few rolls of ribbon to tie some presents. She had 9 presents to tie. She used 1.48 m of ribbon to tie each present. If each roll of ribbon was 5 m long, what was the least number of rolls of ribbon Andrea had to buy?

5. After buying 7 shirts, each of which costs $18.95 at a sale, Laura has $12.55 left. How much money did he have at first?

6. A grocer had 29.2 kg of rice. He packed them into 8 bags of equal weight and had 1.2 kg of rice left. How much did each bag of rice weigh?

7. A watermelon weighs 5.42 kg. It is $1\frac{1}{2}$ kg heavier than a pineapple. How much do the two fruits weigh altogether?

8. Mrs. Ho wants to lay carpet in her bedroom, measuring 5.6 m by 4 m. How much will it cost to lay carpet in the room if the cost of laying the carpet is $25 per square meter?

9. Mohammed weighs 31.68 kg. Alan weighs 6.5 kg more than Mohammed. Nickey weighs $27\frac{1}{2}$ kg. How much do the three boys weigh altogether?

10. Sammy and Tony have $9 altogether. Tony has 0.7 of the total sum of money. How much more money does Tony have than Sammy, correct to the nearest dollar?

11. The table below shows the price of some food items in a supermarket.

Food item	Price
Eggs	12 for $1.75
Oranges	3 for $1.80
Pears	2 for $0.95
Prawns	$1.90 for 4 oz
Live Crabs	$25 each

Mrs. De Souza bought 36 eggs, 10 pears and 1.5 lb of prawns. How much change did she get if she gave two 20-dollar bills to the cashier?

12. Jason, Joel and John share $100.80. Joel has $3.45 more than Jason. John has three times as much money as Joel.
    (a) How much does Joel have?
    (b) How much less money does Jason have than John?

13. Miss Tay paid a total of $14.00 for 5 mangoes and 8 oranges. Each mango cost $1.50 more than an orange. Find the cost of each mango and each orange.

14. On a particular day, Mr. Lee rewarded his class for doing well in the mathematics exam. He bought each student an order of fries and a burger. An order of fries cost $1.02 and a burger cost 98 cents. He paid $76 in total. How many students are there in Mr. Lee's class, if 2 students were absent on that day?

15. Jasmine bought 7 more fifty-cent stamps than twenty-cent stamps. She paid $9.10 for all the stamps. How many stamps did she buy?

Take the **Challenge!**

1. Using $\frac{1}{5} = 0.2$, $\frac{1}{50} = 0.02$ and $\frac{1}{500} = 0.002$, find the value of $\frac{111}{500}$.

   Give the answer as a decimal.

2. Peanuts are sold at $6 per kg.
   Cashew nuts are sold at $12 per kg.
   How many kilograms of cashew nuts are needed to mix with 12 kg of peanuts to obtain a mixture selling at $8.40 per kg?

3. On a test containing 40 math problems, a score of 2.5 is given for each correct answer and 1 is taken away for each incorrect answer. If Thea scored 75.5 how many problems did she answer correctly?

1. Fill in the blanks.

   (a)   3 m 84 cm = _____ cm

   (b)   300 cm = _____ m

   (c)   703 cm = _____ m _____ cm

   (d)   1 km 273 m = _____ m

   (e)   5 km = _____ m

   (f)   4070 m = _____ km _____ m

   (g)   6 kg 575 g = _____ g

   (h)   7000 g = _____ kg

   (i)   9304 g = _____ kg _____ g

   (j)   5026 ml = _____ ℓ _____ ml

   (k)   2000 ml = _____ ℓ

   (l)   6 ℓ 493 ml = _____ ml

   (m)   112 in. = _____ ft _____ in.

   (n)   15 yd = _____ ft

   (o)   400 qt = _____ gal

   (p)   22 c = _____ qt _____ c

   (q)   9 lb = _____ oz

   (r)   33 oz = _____ lb _____ oz

2. Fill in the blanks.

    (a)   3 h = _____ min

    (b)   1 h 25 min = _____ min

    (c)   240 min = _____ h

    (d)   138 min = _____ h _____ min

    (e)   120 s = _____ min

    (f)   203 s = _____ min _____ s

    (g)   8 min = _____ s

    (h)   2 min 39 s = _____ s

3. Multiply and give the answers in compound units.

    (a)   3 m 63 cm × 6 =   (b)   7 km 83 m × 4 =

    (c)   3 h 43 min × 5 =   (d)   12 min 8 s × 7 =

    (e)   5 ft 8 in. × 9 =   (f)   8 gal 3 qt × 7 =

4. Divide and give the answers in compound units.

   (a)   12 m 48 cm ÷ 8 =   (b)   40 km 691 m ÷ 7 =

   (c)   6 kg 54 g ÷ 3 =   (d)   10 ℓ 197 ml ÷ 9 =

   (e)   20 h 55 min ÷ 5 =   (f)   10 ft 6 in ÷ 6 =

5. Express each measurement given in compound units as a decimal of the greater unit.

(Use the concept of place values in the conversion.)

Example 1:

5 km 45 m = 5045 m = 5.045 km

Example 2:

2 m 13 cm = 213 cm = 2.13 m

(a)   4 m 85 cm = _____ m

(b)   15 km 264 m = _____ km

(c)   3 kg 455 g = _____ kg

(d)   1 ℓ 890 ml = _____ ℓ

(e)   14,565 cents = $ _____

(f)   11 kg 35 g = _____ kg

WORD PROBLEMS

1. Nellie bought 6 cartons of guava juice from the supermarket. Each carton contained 1 ℓ 890 ml of guava juice. How much guava juice was there altogether?

2. Ahmad bought a 10-kg bag of rice. He used some of the rice and repacked the remaining 8 kg 624 g of rice into 8 smaller bags, each containing equal amount of rice. How much rice was there in each bag?

3. Some meat is sold in a supermarket at $4 per pound. Mrs. Lee bought 3 lb 14 oz of the meat. How much did she pay for the meat?

4. A piece of wire, 8 m 28 cm long, is cut into 3 pieces. The first piece is twice as long as the second piece and the third piece is three times as long as the second piece. Find the length of the second piece.

5. Tom works at a gas station. He works from 7:30 am to 5:00 pm daily from Monday to Saturday. Tom's hourly wage is $6.
    (a) What is his total working hours in a week?
    (b) How much does he earn in a week?

6. Cecilia's car used 2 gallons of gas for every 15 mi travelled. How much would Cecilia spend on gas for a journey of 300 mi, if 1 gallon of gas cost $1.19?

7. A watermelon weighs 5 kg 420 g. A mango weighs $\frac{1}{5}$ as much.
    (a) How heavy is a mango?
    (b) How much will 3 such watermelons and 6 such mangoes weigh altogether?

8. A seamstress bought a roll of cloth. She cut 4 pieces of cloth to make blouses. Each piece was 1 yd 17 in. long. After that, she cut the remaining roll of cloth into 5 pieces to make skirts. Each of these pieces was 2 yd 8 in. long.
    (a)   What is the length of the entire roll of cloth?
    (b)   If the seamstress paid $10.50 per yard for the roll of cloth, how much did the roll of cloth cost?

9. Daisy packed 485 g of peanut butter into each of 8 jars and had 1 kg 650 g of peanut butter left. How many kilograms of peanut butter did Daisy have at first?

10. All the wine from a barrel is poured into 3 containers. The first container holds 17 ℓ 460 ml of wine and the second container holds three times as much wine as the first container. The third container holds $\frac{1}{2}$ as much wine as the second container. How much wine was in the barrel at first?

Topic 4: Symmetry

1. Look at each of the following figures. Check (✓) the box if it is a symmetric figure and cross (✗) the box if it is not.

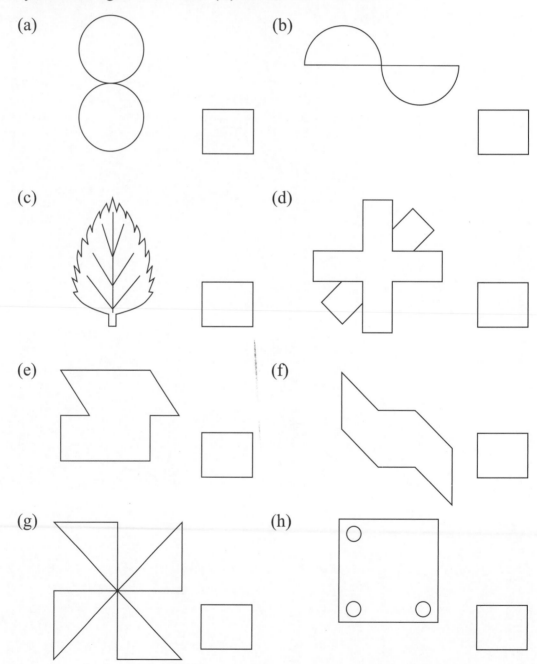

(a)

(b)

(c)

(d)

(e)

(f)

(g)

(h)

2. Match each of the following figures on the left with the correct symmetric figures on the right.

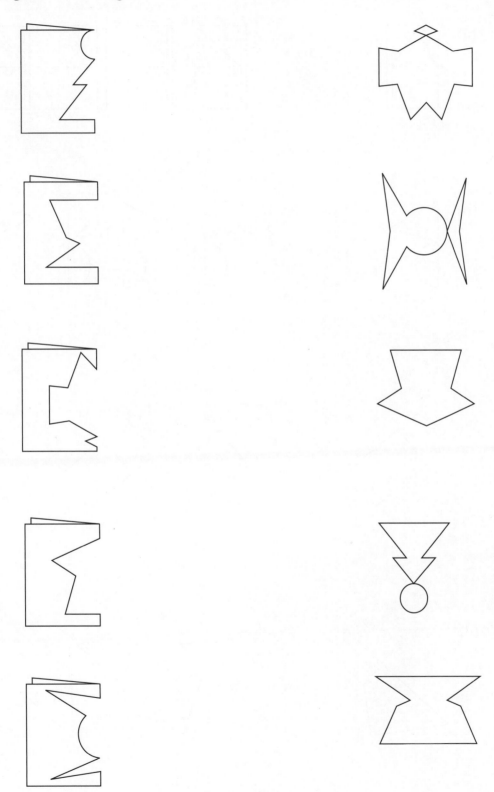

3. Each of the following figures on the left shows half of a symmetric figure. Circle the other half of the figure on the right.

(a)

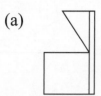 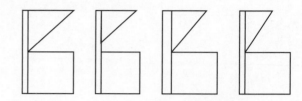

(b)

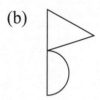 

(c)

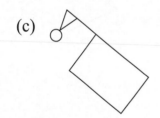 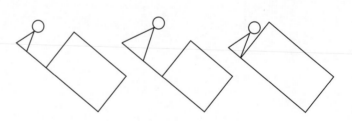

(d)

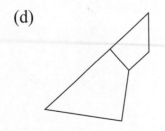 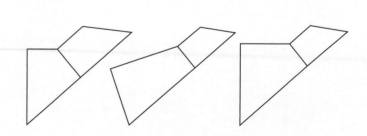

4. In each of the following figures, check (✓) the box if the dotted line is a line of symmetry and cross (✗) the box if it is not.

(a)

(b)

(c)

(d)

(e)

(f)

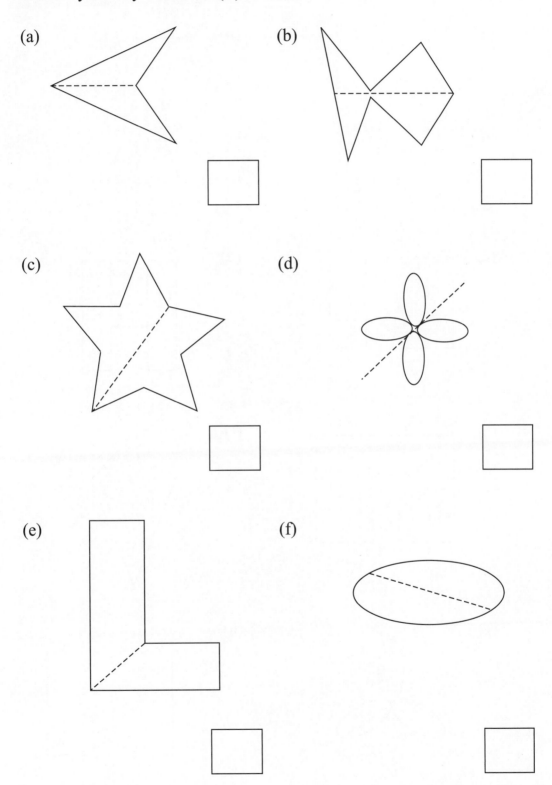

5. Draw as many lines of symmetry as possible in each of the following figures.

(a)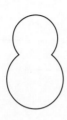

(b)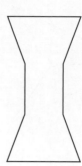

(c)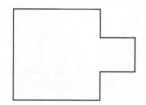

(d)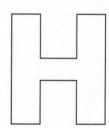

(e)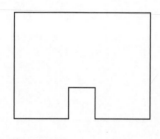

(f)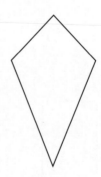

(g)

(h)

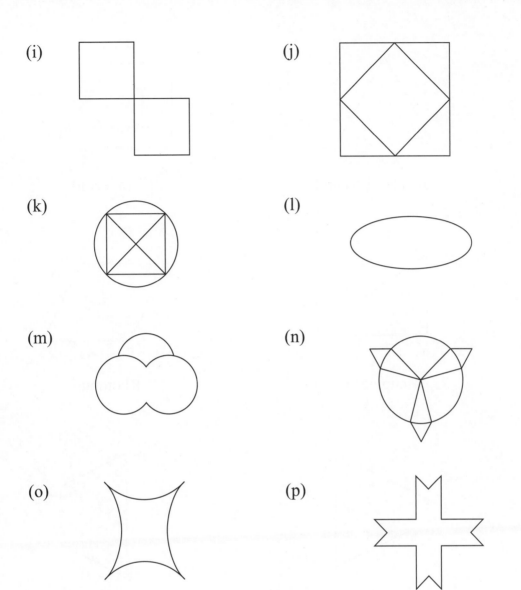

(i)

(j)

(k)

(l)

(m)

(n)

(o)

(p)

6. Draw as many lines of symmetry as possible in each of the following figures.

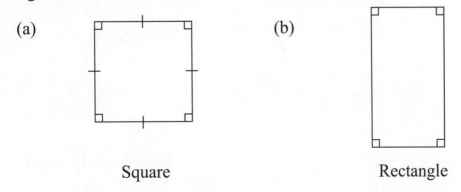

(a)

Square

(b)

Rectangle

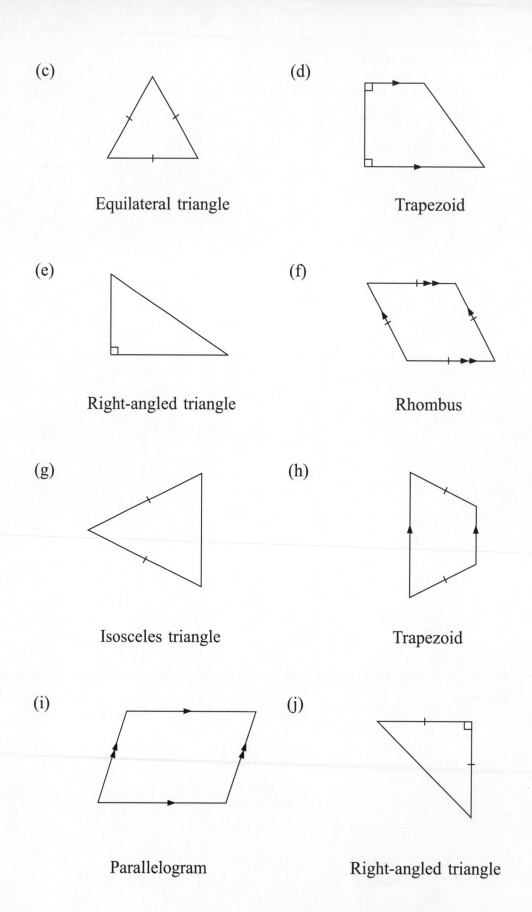

(c)

Equilateral triangle

(d)

Trapezoid

(e)

Right-angled triangle

(f)

Rhombus

(g)

Isosceles triangle

(h)

Trapezoid

(i)

Parallelogram

(j)

Right-angled triangle

7. Each of the following shows half of a symmetric figure.
   Complete each symmetric figure with the dotted line as its line of symmetry.

(a)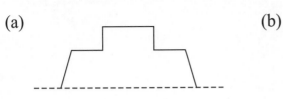

(b)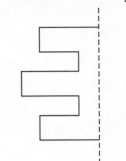

(c)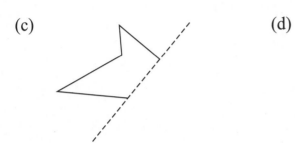

(d)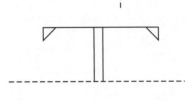

(e)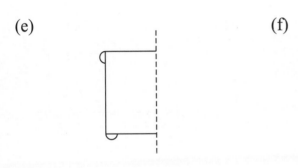

(f)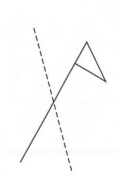

(g)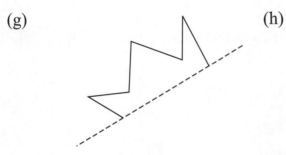

(h)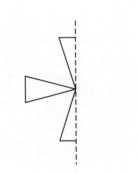

(i)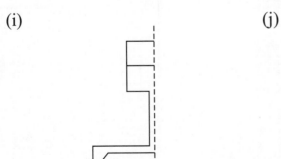

(j)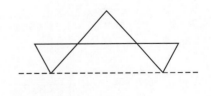

53

(k)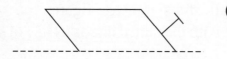

(l)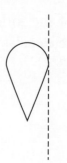

(m)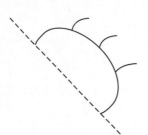

(n)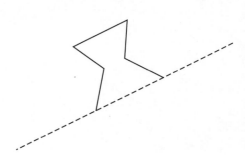

(o)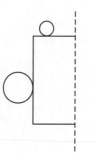

(p)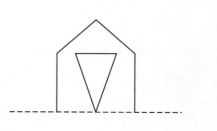

8. Using the dotted line as a line of symmetry, complete each of the following symmetric figures.

(a)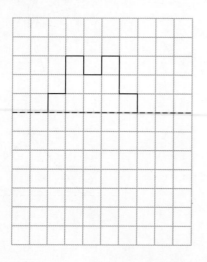

(b)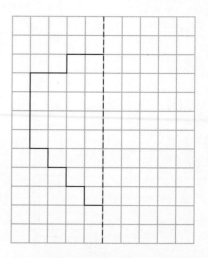

(c)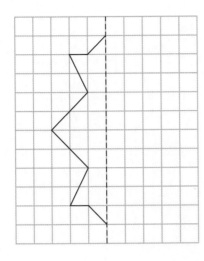

(d)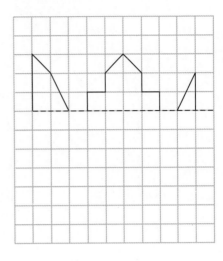

(e)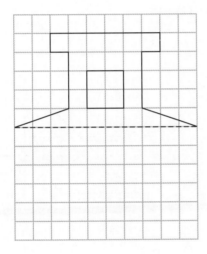

(f)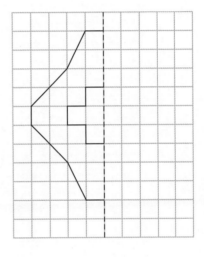

(g)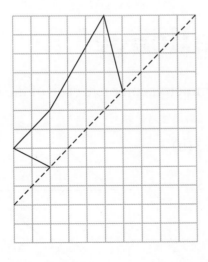

(h)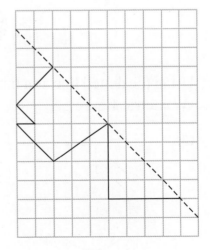

(i)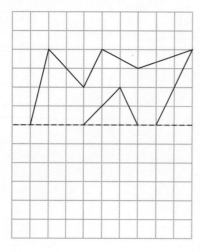

(j)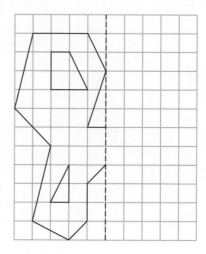

(k)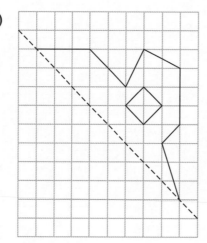

(l)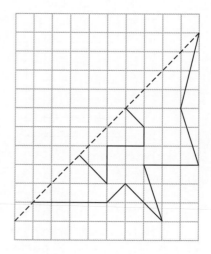

T̢ake the Challenge!

1. Using the dotted line as a line of symmetry, complete each of the following symmetric figures.

(a)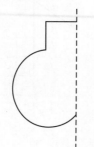

(b)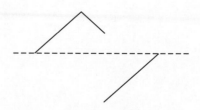

(c)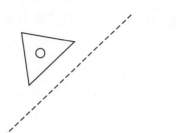

(d)

(e)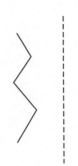

(f)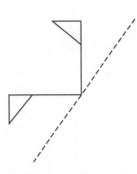

(g)

(h)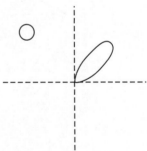

2. Using the dotted line as a line of symmetry, complete each of the following symmetric figures.

(a)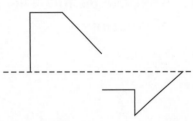

(b)

(c)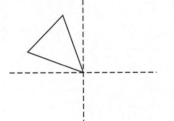

(d)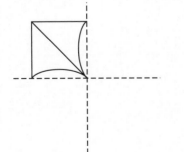

3. The symmetric figure shows a square and a circle. Draw a line of symmetry in the figure.

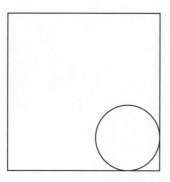

4. Complete the following symmetric figures, using the dotted line as a line of symmetry.

(a)

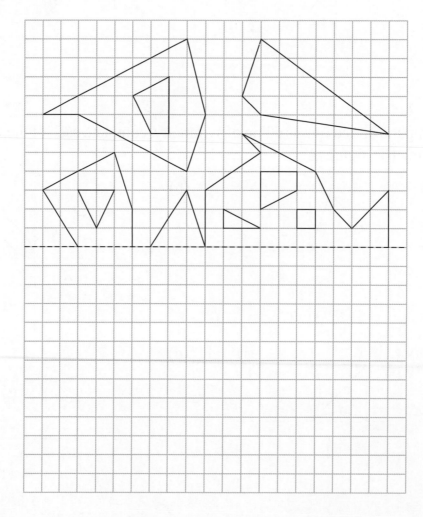

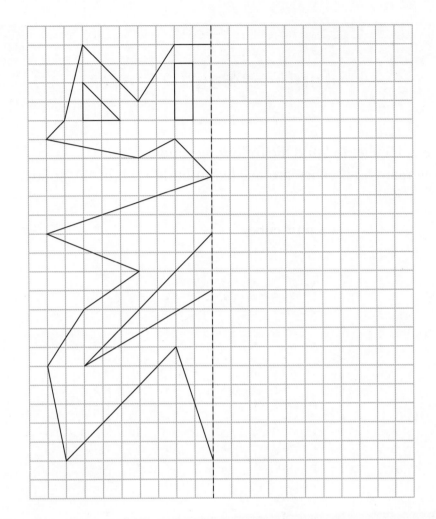

Topic 5: Solid Figures

1. Use unit cubes to build the following solids.
    How many unit cubes are needed to build each of the solids?

     is a unit cube.

    (a)

    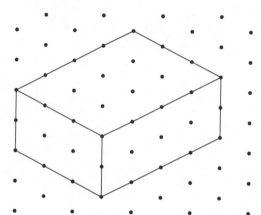

    (b)

    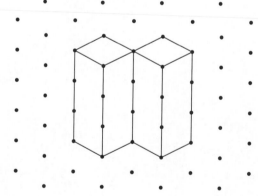

    (c)

    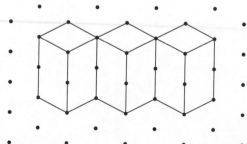

(d)

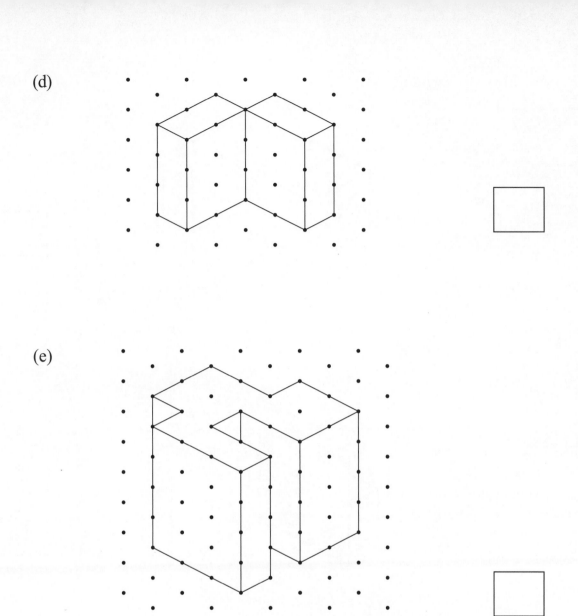

(e)

(f)

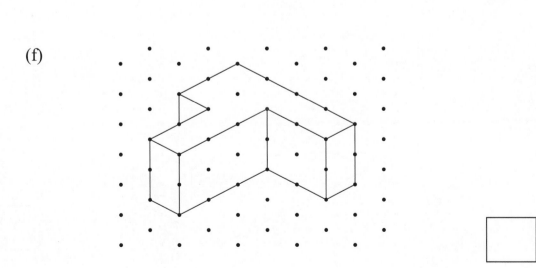

(g)

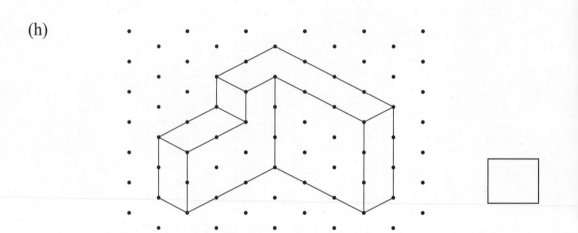

(h)

(i)

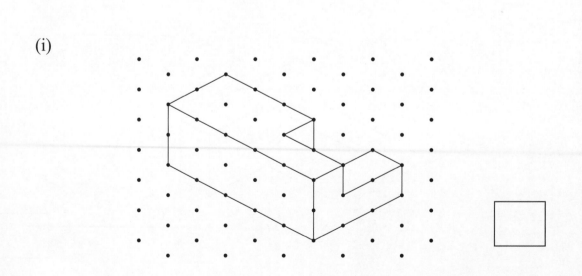

(j)

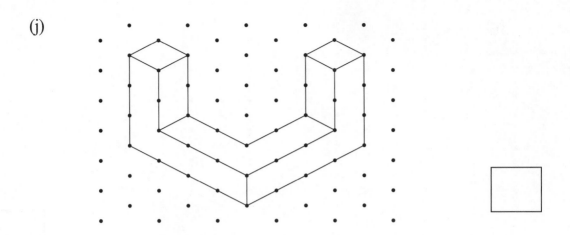

2. Find the number of unit cubes needed to build each of the following solids.

(a)

(b)

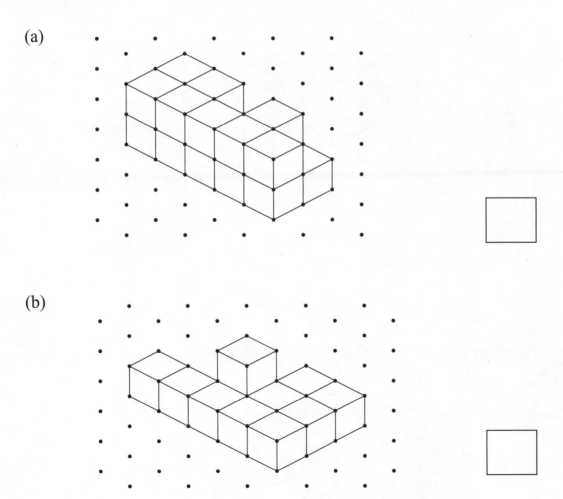

(c)

(d)

(e)

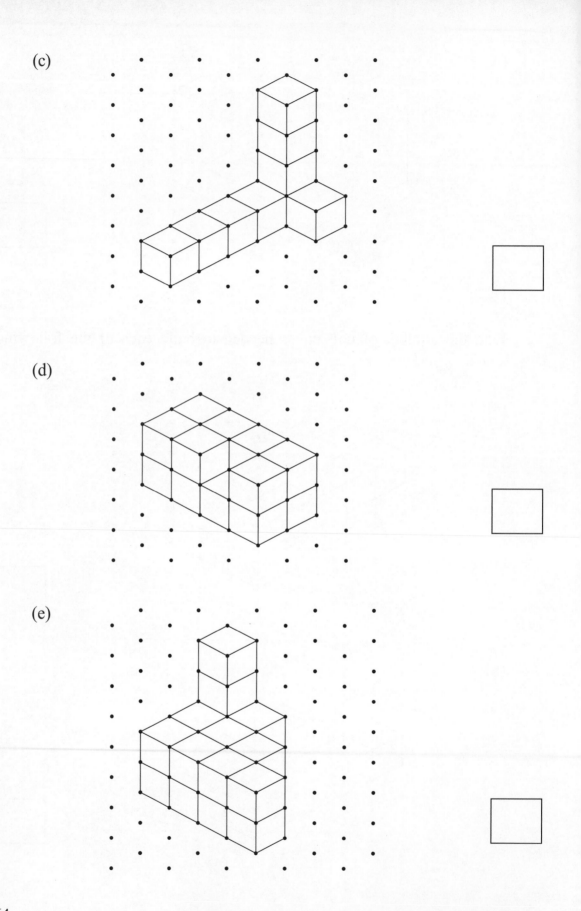

(f)

(g)

(h)

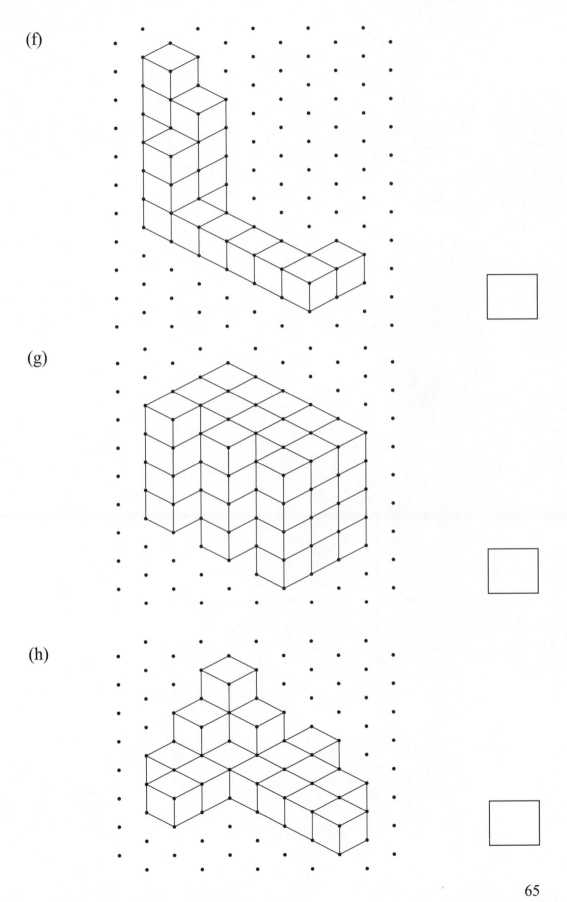

(i)

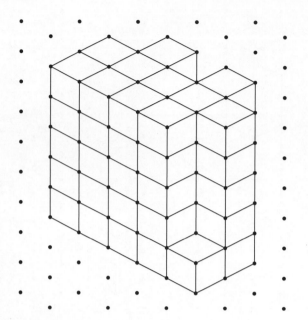

(j)

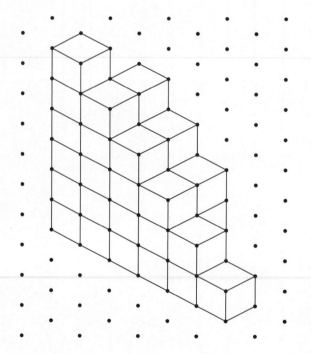

3. Find the number of unit cubes needed to build each of the following solids.

(a)

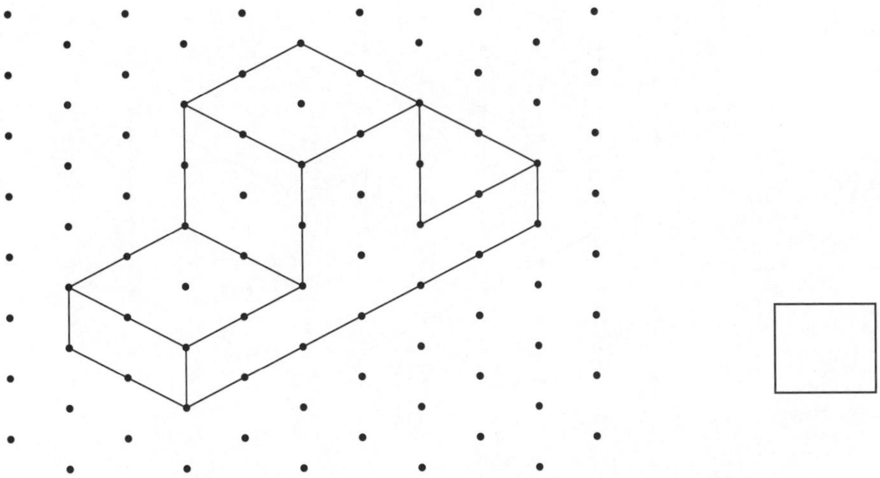

(b)

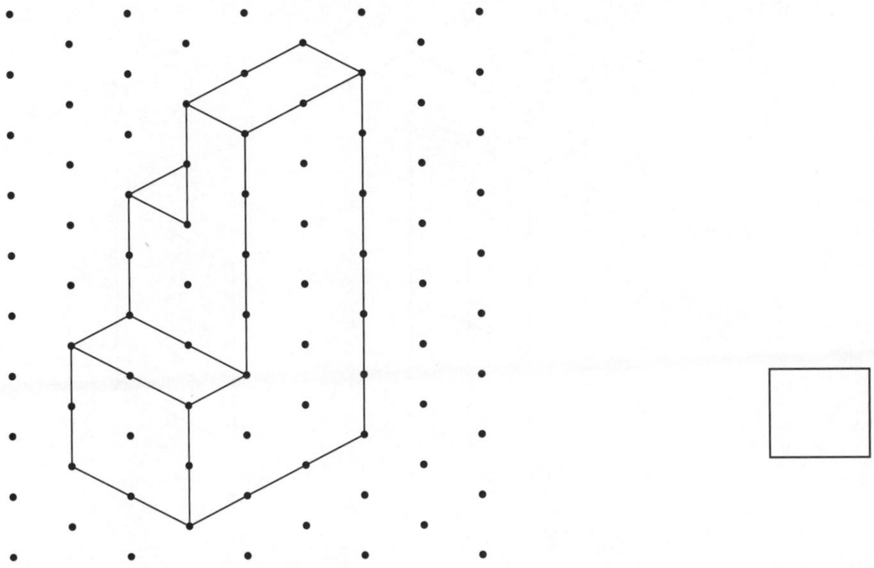

(c)

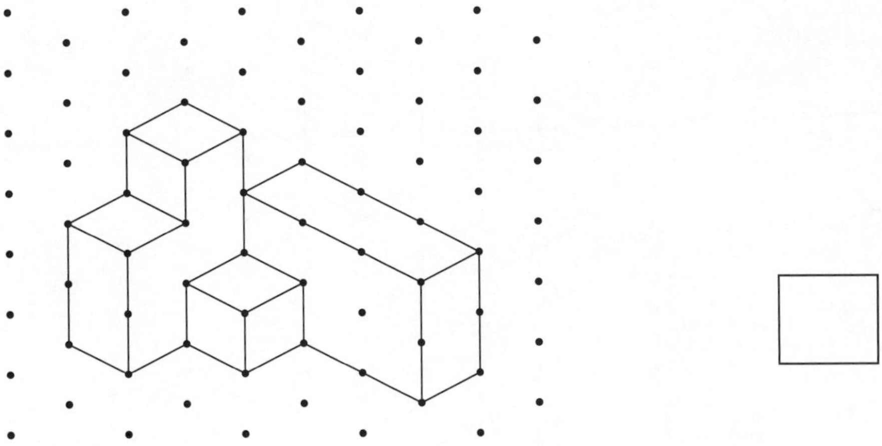

(d)

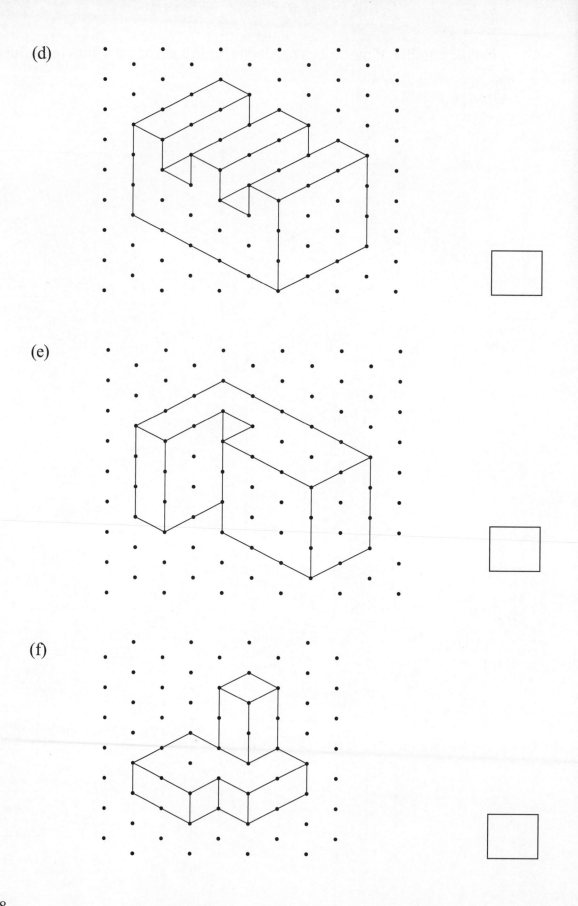

(e)

(f)

68

(g)

(h)

(i)

(j)

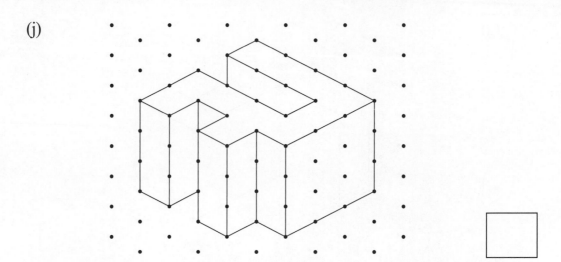

4. Each of the following solids on the left is made up of unit cubes.
   Some unit cubes are removed to get the solid on the right. How many unit
   cubes are removed in each case?

(a)

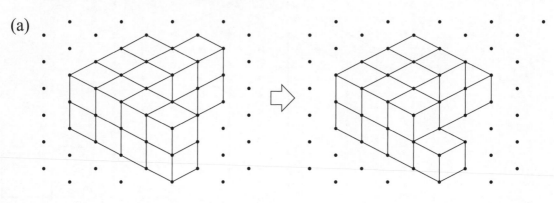

(b)

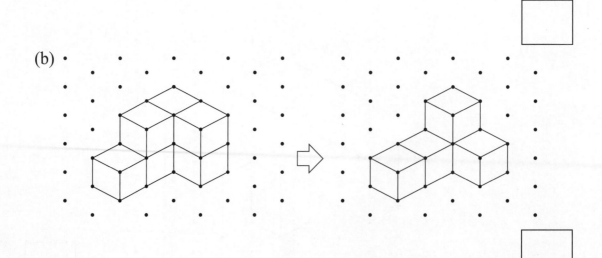

(c)

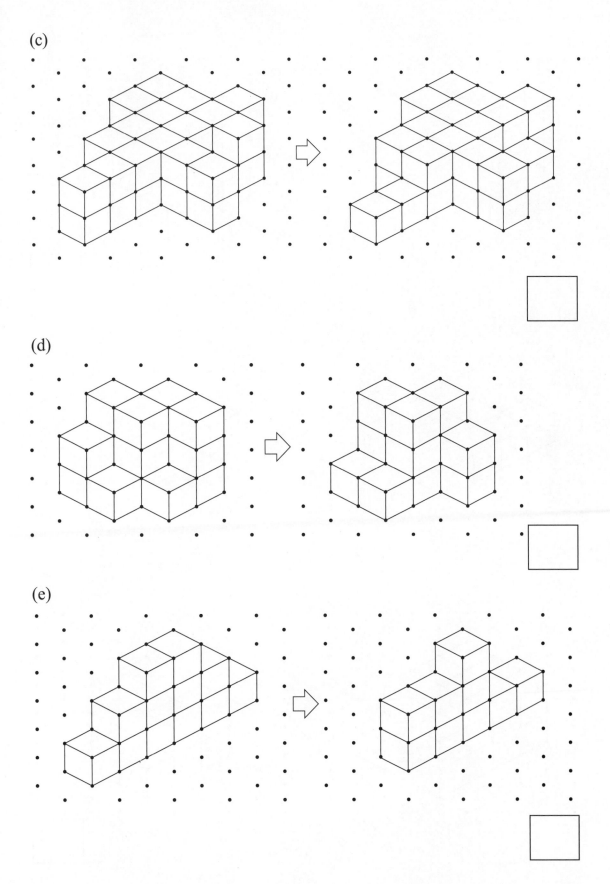

(d)

(e)

71

(f)

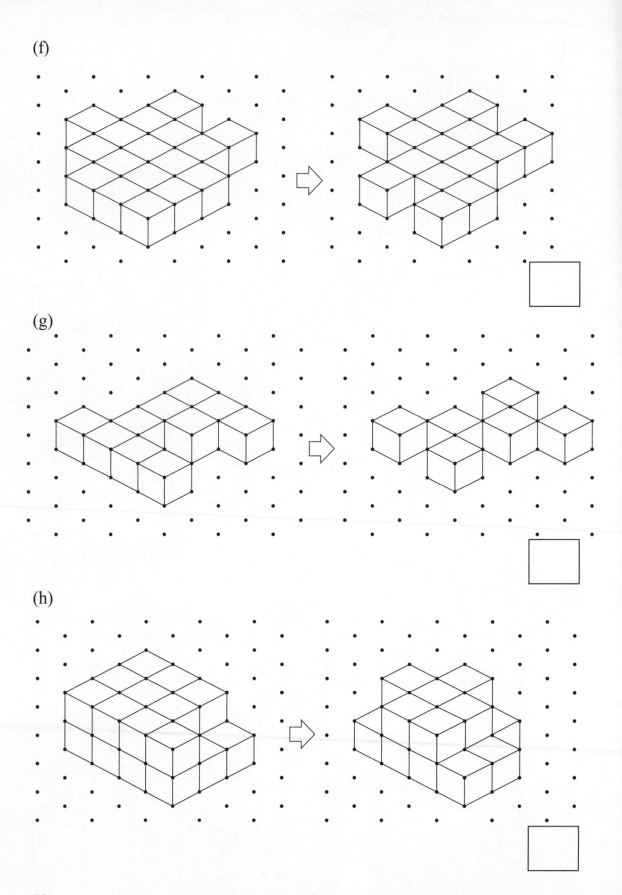

(g)

(h)

72

5. Each of the following solids on the left is made up of unit cubes.
   Some unit cubes are added to get the solid on the right. How many unit cubes are added in each case?

(a)

(b)

(c)

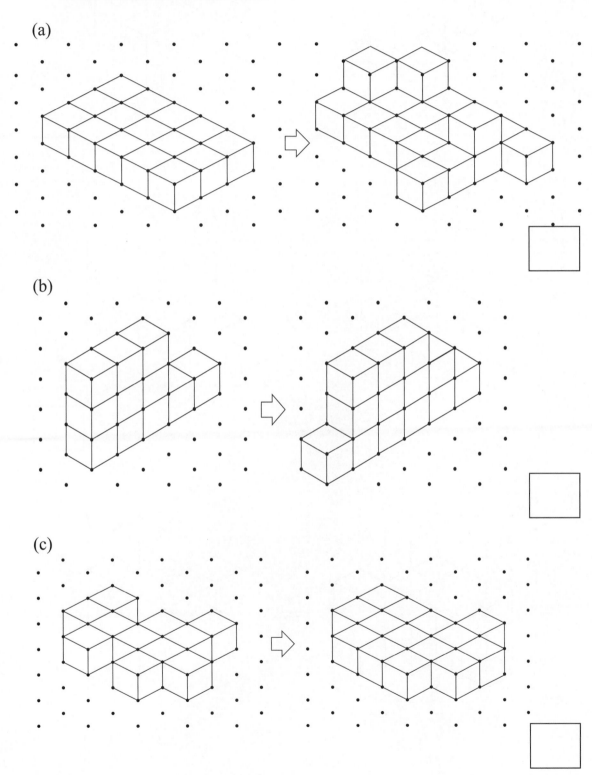

(d)

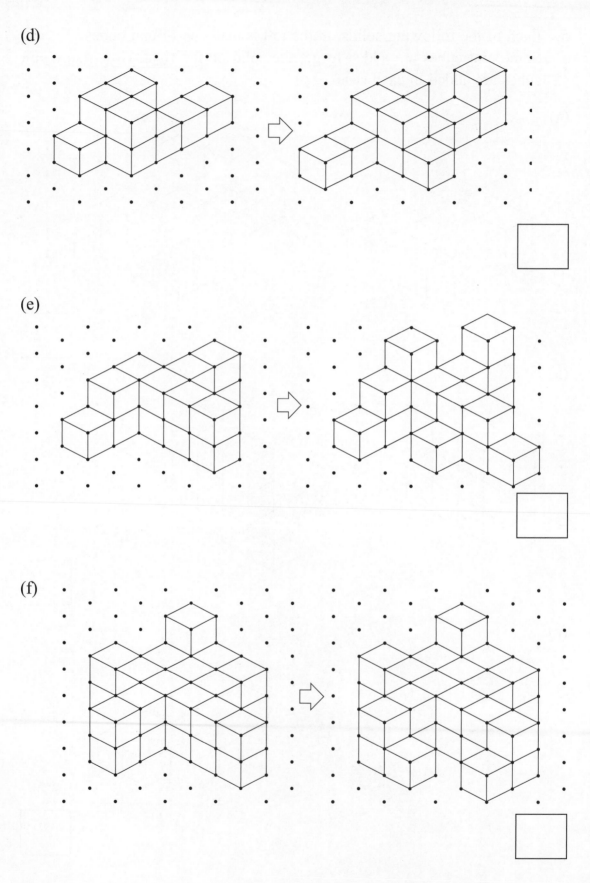

(e)

(f)

(g)

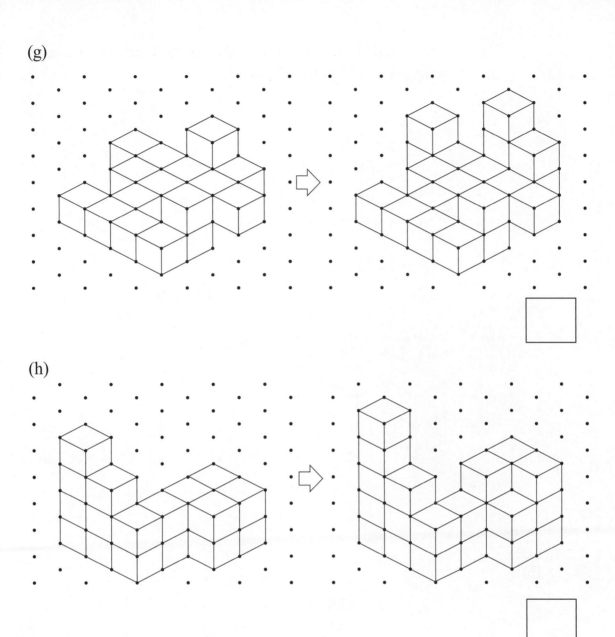

(h)

6. Each of the following solids is made up of unit cubes.

(a)

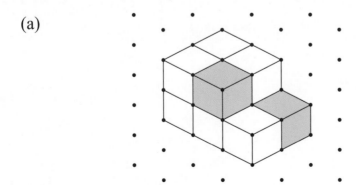

When the two shaded cubes are removed from the solid, which one of the following solids will you see? Circle it.

(i) 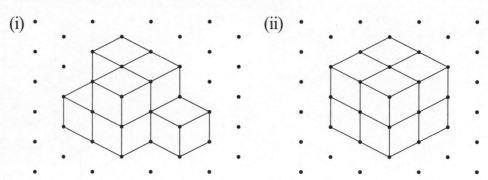 (ii)

(iii) 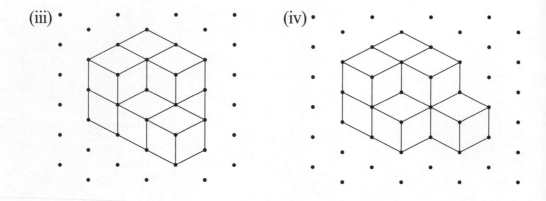 (iv)

(b)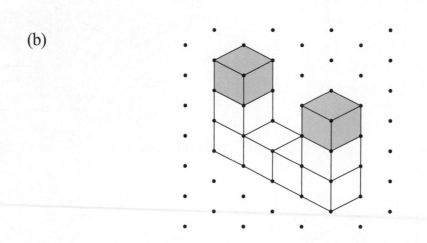

When the two shaded cubes are removed from the solid, which one of the following solids will you see? Circle it.

(i)

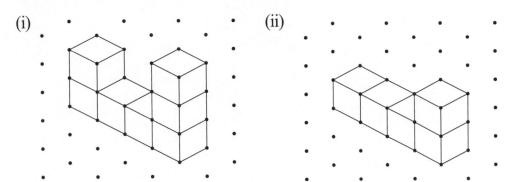

(ii)

(iii)

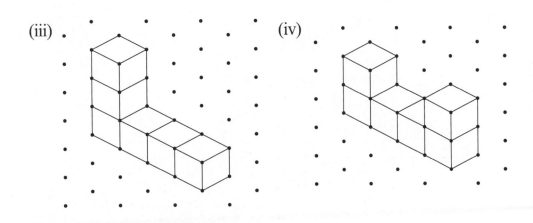

(iv)

(c)

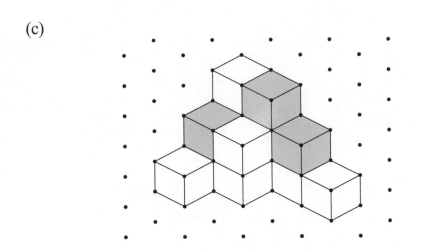

When the three shaded cubes are removed from the solid, which one of the following solids will you see? Circle it.

(i)

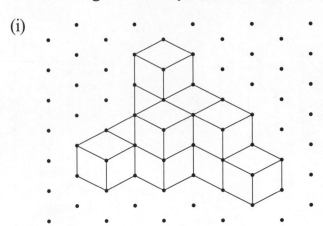

(ii)

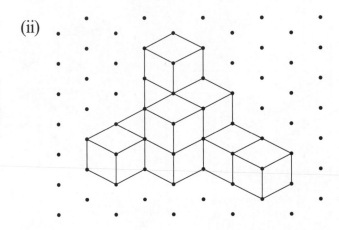

(iii)

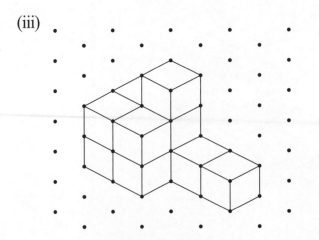

(iv)

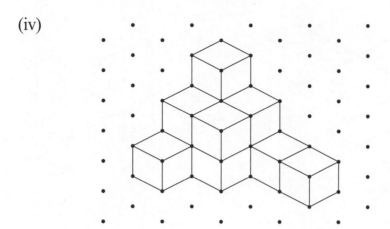

Take the Challenge!

1. Each of the following solids on the left is made up of unit cubes.
   Some unit cubes are removed to get the solid on the right. State the
   number of unit cubes that are removed in each case.

(a)

(b)

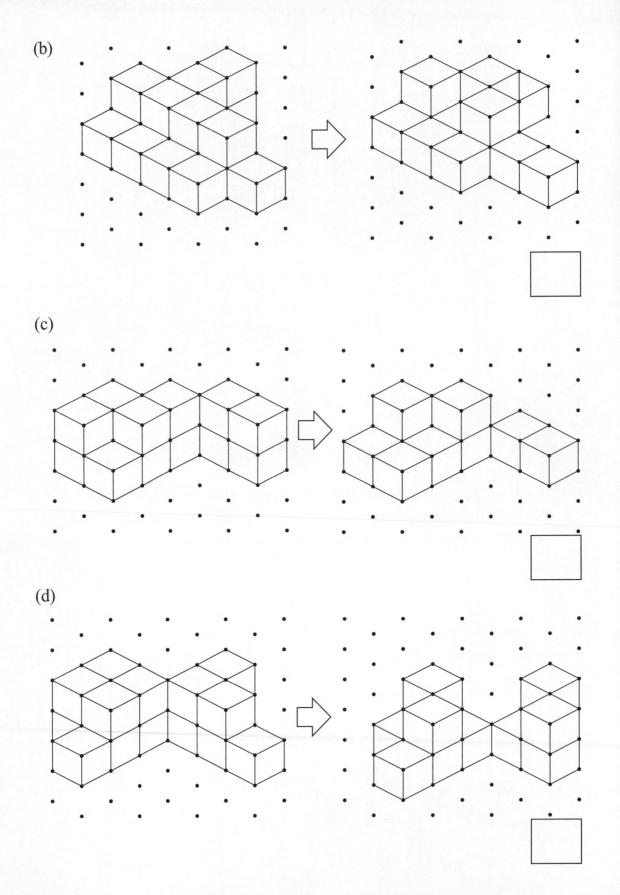

(c)

(d)

2. Each of the following solids on the left is made up of unit cubes.
   Some unit cubes are added to get the solid on the right. State the number
   of unit cubes that are added in each case.

(a)

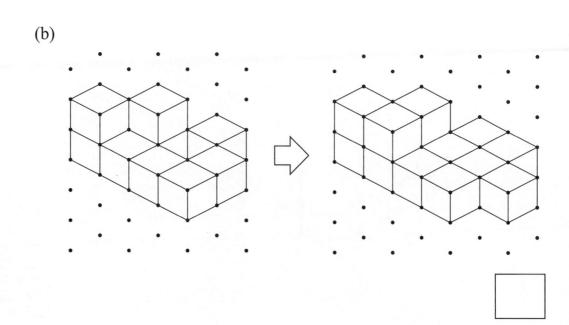

(b)

(c)

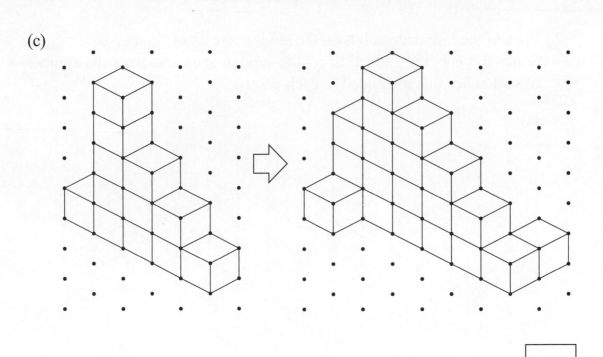

(d)

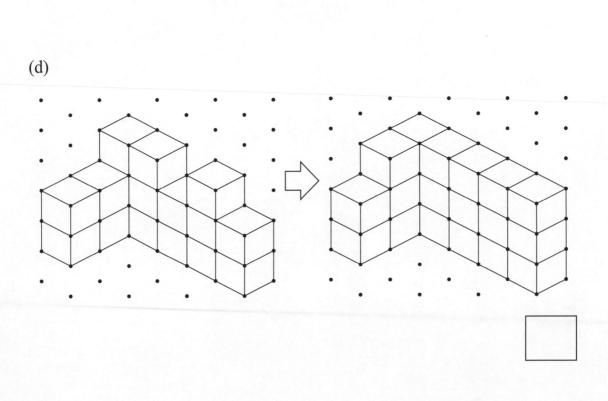

Topic 6: Volume

1. Find the volume of each of the following solids.

(a)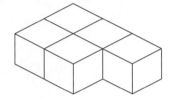

[ ] cubic units

(b)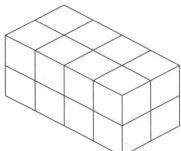

[ ] cubic units

(c)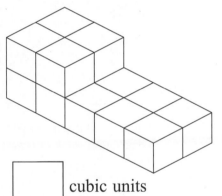

[ ] cubic units

(d)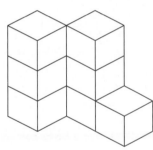

[ ] cubic units

(e)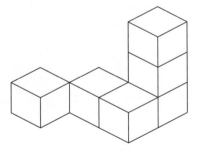

[ ] cubic units

(f)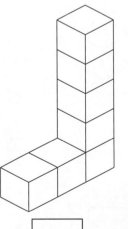

[ ] cubic units

(g)

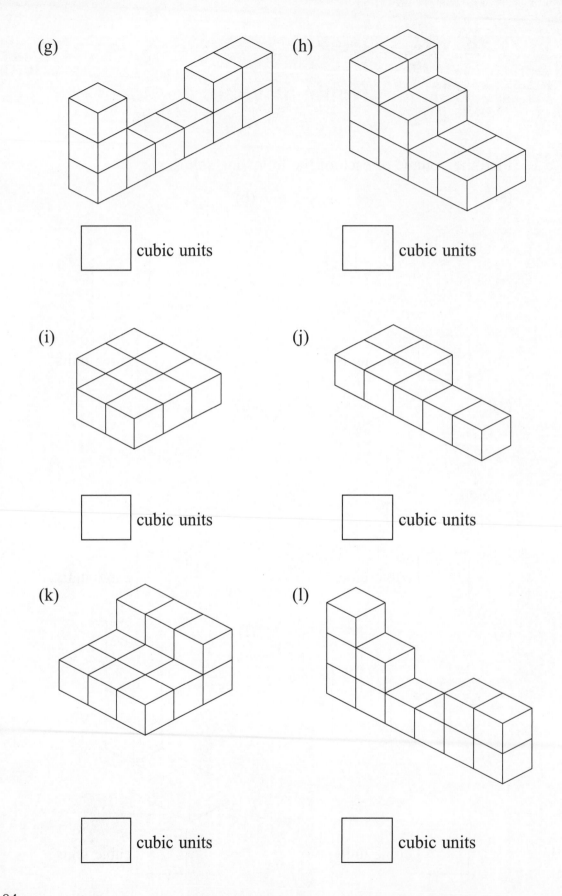

(h)

☐ cubic units   ☐ cubic units

(i)

(j)

☐ cubic units   ☐ cubic units

(k)

(l)

☐ cubic units   ☐ cubic units

2. Each of the following solids is made up of 1-cm cubes. Find the volume of each solid.

(a)

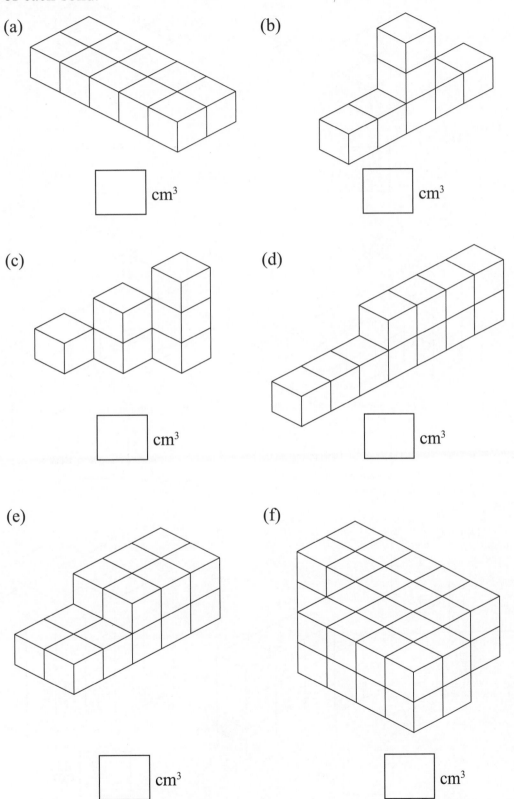

$\boxed{}$ cm³

(b)

$\boxed{}$ cm³

(c)

$\boxed{}$ cm³

(d)

$\boxed{}$ cm³

(e)

$\boxed{}$ cm³

(f)

$\boxed{}$ cm³

(g)

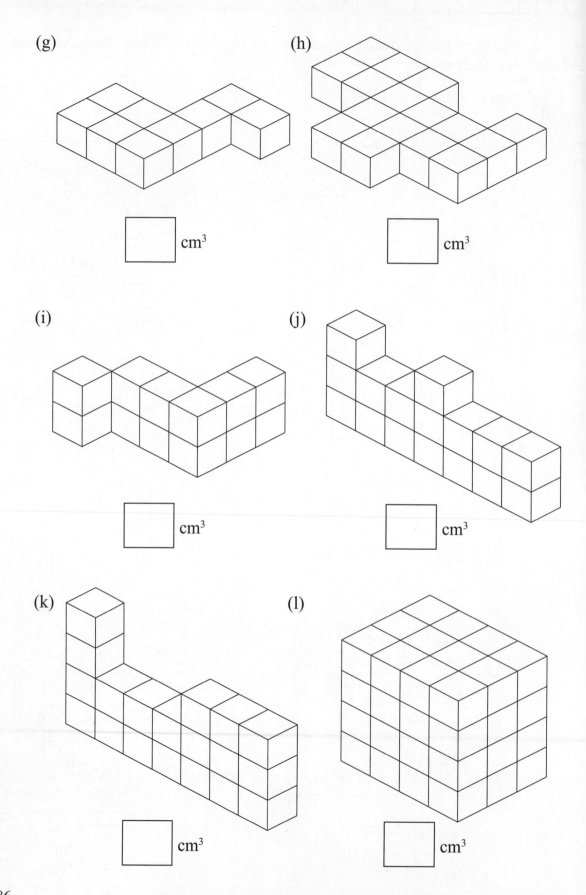

cm³

(h)

cm³

(i)

cm³

(j)

cm³

(k)

cm³

(l)

cm³

3. Each of the following cuboids is made up of 1-cm cubes. Find the length, width, height and volume of each cuboid.

(a)

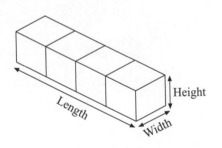

(b)

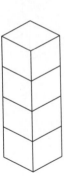

Length = _____

Width = _____

Height = _____

Volume = _____

Length = _____

Width= _____

Height = _____

Volume = _____

(c)

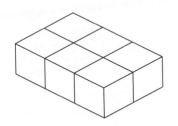

(d)

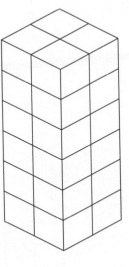

Length = _____

Width = _____

Height = _____

Volume = _____

Length = _____

Width = _____

Height = _____

Volume = _____

(e)

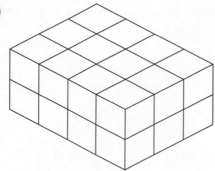

Length   = _____

Width   = _____

Height   = _____

Volume = _____

(f)

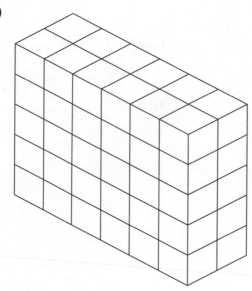

Length   = _____

Width   = _____

Height   = _____

Volume = _____

(g)

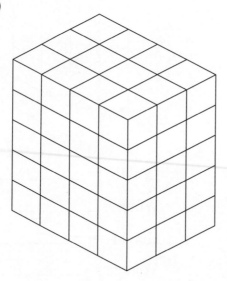

Length   = _____

Width   = _____

Height   = _____

Volume = _____

(h)

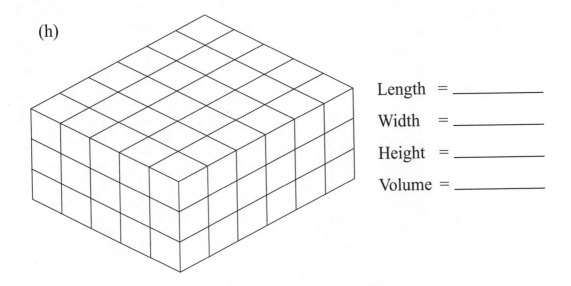

Length = _____

Width   = _____

Height = _____

Volume = _____

4. Find the volume of each of the following cuboids.

(a)

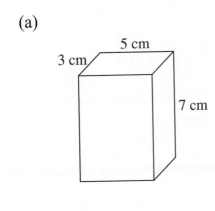

_____

(b)

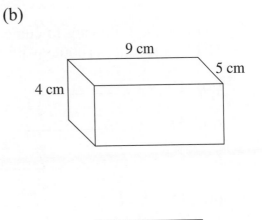

_____

(c)

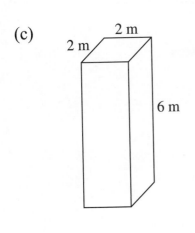

_____

(d)

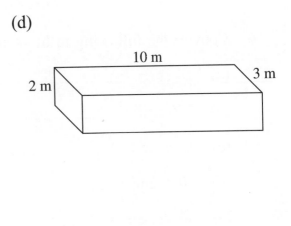

_____

(e)

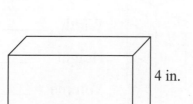

4 in.

2 in.

7 in.

(f)

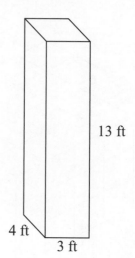

13 ft

4 ft

3 ft

_____   _____

5. Convert the following to cubic centimeters.
   (1 ℓ = 1000 ml = 1000 cm³)

   (a) 1 ℓ = _____   (b) 562 ml = _____

   (c) 38 ℓ = _____   (d) 73 ml = _____

   (e) 6 ℓ 520 ml = _____   (f) $\frac{1}{2}$ ml = _____

   (g) 15 ℓ 5 ml = _____   (h) 3 ℓ 60 ml = _____

   (i) 0.8 ℓ = _____   (j) 0.3 ℓ = _____

6. Convert the following to liters and milliliters.

   (a) 19 cm³ = _____

   (b) 275 cm³ = _____

   (c) 1598 cm³ = _____

   (d) 8095 cm³ = _____

   (e) 36,427 cm³ = _____

(f) $0.72 \text{ cm}^3 =$ _____

(g) $206{,}381 \text{ cm}^3 =$ _____

(h) $10{,}058 \text{ cm}^3 =$ _____

(i) $1000.2 \text{ cm}^3 =$ _____

(j) $38.5 \text{ cm}^3 =$ _____

7. Find the volume of the water in milliliters.
    ($1 \text{ ml} = 1 \text{ cm}^3$)

(a)

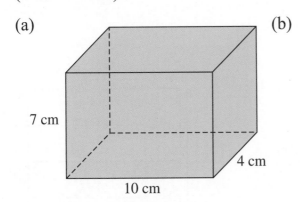

7 cm

10 cm   4 cm

_____

(b)

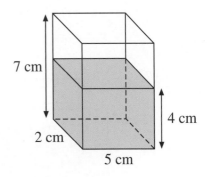

7 cm

2 cm   4 cm

5 cm

_____

(c)

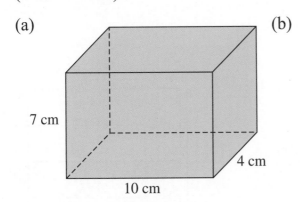

10 cm

17 cm

7 cm

8 cm

_____

(d)

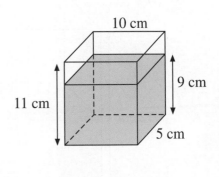

10 cm

11 cm   9 cm

5 cm

_____

(e)

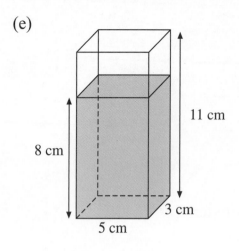

11 cm

8 cm

3 cm

5 cm

_____

(f)

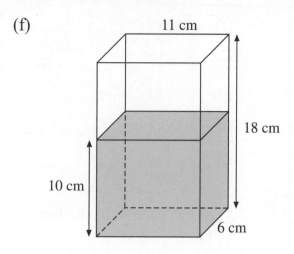

11 cm

18 cm

10 cm

6 cm

_____

(g)

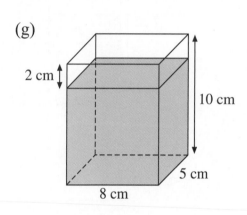

2 cm

10 cm

5 cm

8 cm

_____

(h)

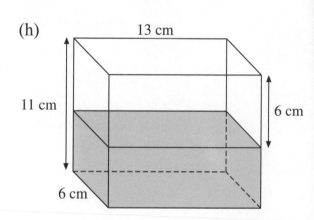

13 cm

11 cm

6 cm

6 cm

_____

(i)

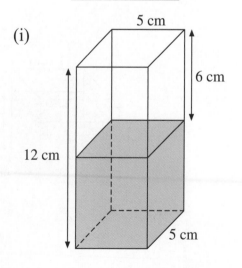

5 cm

6 cm

12 cm

5 cm

_____

(j)

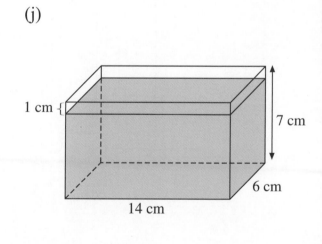

1 cm {

7 cm

6 cm

14 cm

_____

(k)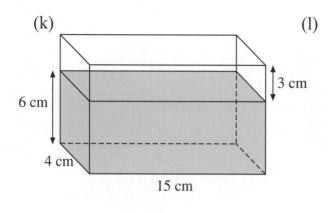

3 cm

6 cm

4 cm

15 cm

_____

(l)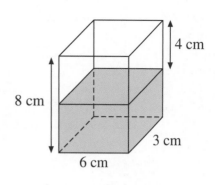

4 cm

8 cm

3 cm

6 cm

_____

8. Find the volume of the water in liters.
   (1 ℓ = 1000 cm³)

(a)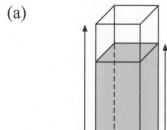

63 cm

50 cm

12 cm

5 cm

_____

(b)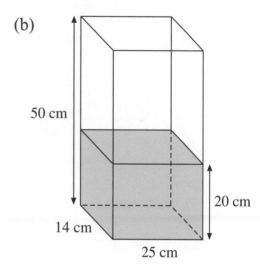

50 cm

14 cm

20 cm

25 cm

_____

(c)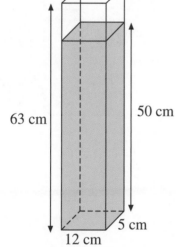

40 cm

20 cm

20 cm

_____

(d)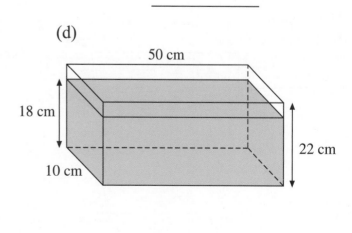

50 cm

18 cm

10 cm

22 cm

_____

(e)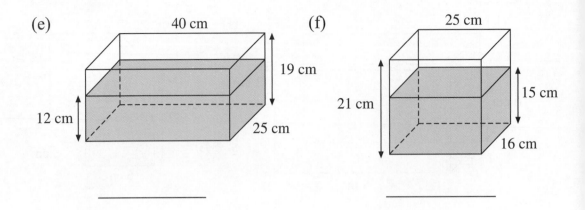

40 cm

19 cm

12 cm

25 cm

_____

(f)

25 cm

21 cm

15 cm

16 cm

_____

(g)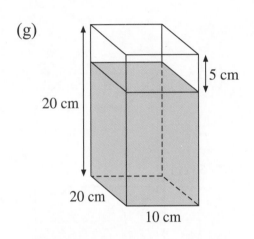

20 cm

5 cm

20 cm

10 cm

_____

(h)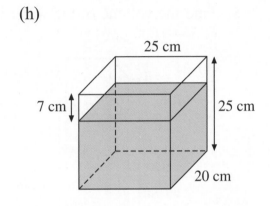

25 cm

7 cm

25 cm

20 cm

_____

(i)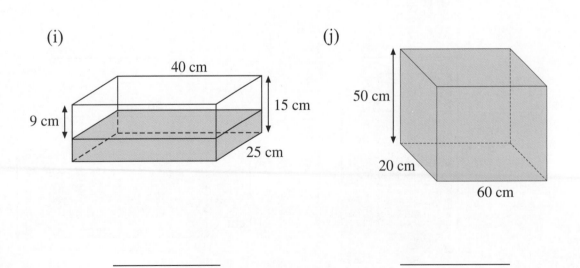

40 cm

15 cm

9 cm

25 cm

_____

(j)

50 cm

20 cm

60 cm

_____

(k)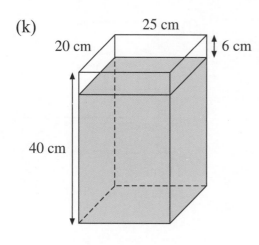

(l)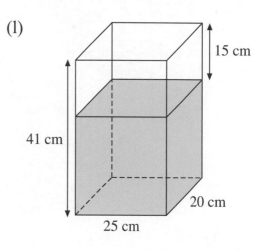

9. Find the volume of the water in liters and milliliters.

(a)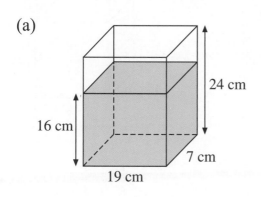

(b)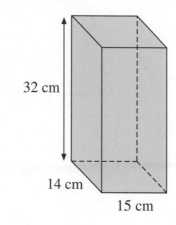

(c)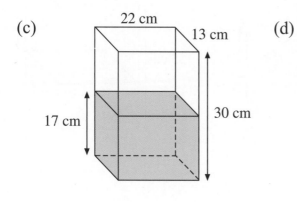

(d)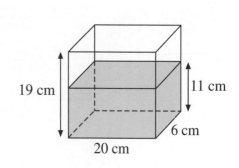

(e)

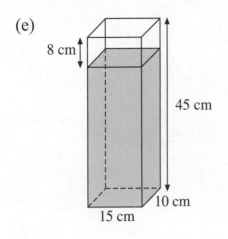

8 cm

45 cm

10 cm

15 cm

_____

(f)

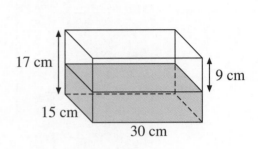

17 cm

9 cm

15 cm

30 cm

_____

(g)

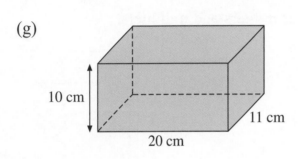

10 cm

20 cm

11 cm

_____

(h)

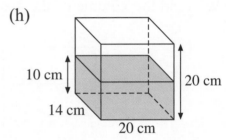

10 cm

20 cm

14 cm

20 cm

_____

(i)

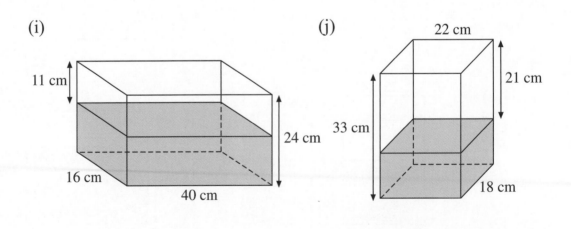

11 cm

24 cm

16 cm

40 cm

_____

(j)

22 cm

21 cm

33 cm

18 cm

_____

(k)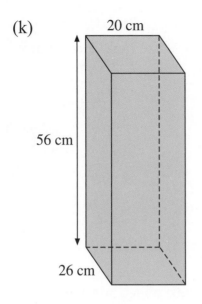

20 cm

56 cm

26 cm

_____

(l)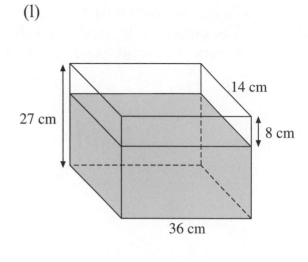

14 cm

27 cm

8 cm

36 cm

_____

WORD PROBLEMS

1. A rectangular tank measures 15 cm by 10 cm by 7 cm. It is filled with water to a depth of 5 cm. How many cubic centimeters of water are there in the tank?

2. Sand is poured into a rectangular tank measuring 16 m by 15 m by 18 m. The surface of the sand is 3 m from the top of the tank. How many cubic meters of sand are there in the tank?

3. Water runs from a tap into a rectangular tank which measures 50 cm by 40 cm by 40 cm until it completely fills the tank. How many liters of water are there in the tank?

4. Sally's rectangular fish tank measures 35 cm by 25 cm by 20 cm. She fills the tank with water up to a height of 10 cm. Find the volume of water in the tank in liters and milliliters.

5. Water is poured into a rectangular tank measuring 38 cm by 30 cm by 25 cm until the water reaches a height of 20 cm. The tank is then filled with 700 ml of water. Find the total volume of water in the tank in liters and milliliters.

6. A rectangular tin measures 20 cm by 15 cm by 10 cm. How many liters of water can it hold?

7. A rectangular tank is 30 cm long, 20 cm wide and 28 cm high. It is filled with water to a depth of 21 cm. Some water is then poured away, leaving the water with a depth of 16 cm. How much water, in milliliters, is poured away?

8. A rectangular container measures 18 cm by 15 cm by 12 cm. When 3500 ml of water is poured into the container, some water overflows from the container. Find the volume of water, in milliliters, that overflows.

9. A rectangular tank measuring 35 cm by 14 cm by 10 cm is completely filled with sand. The sand is then poured equally into 7 buckets. If the volume of each bucket is 1 ℓ, find the volume of the space, in liters, in each bucket that is not filled by the sand.

10. A rectangular container with a base measuring 24 cm by 20 cm and a height measuring 16 cm is filled with orange juice to a height of 14 cm. 220 ml of the orange juice is used to mix with other juices. The remaining orange juice is shared among 25 children. If each child can only drink 200 ml of orange juice, how much cubic centimeters of orange juice is left in the container?

Take the Challenge!

1. I have 6 ice cubes in a glass. Each ice cube is of side 3 cm. Find the volume of the water in the glass, in milliliters, when the ice cubes melt.

2.

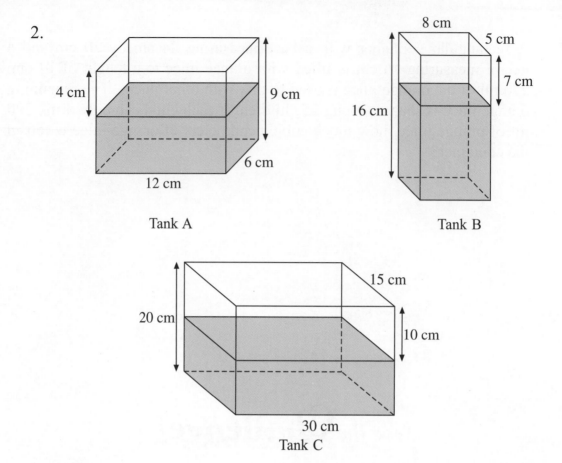

Tank A

Tank B

Tank C

Look at the tanks above. Each tank is filled with water as shown. The water in Tank A and Tank B is then completely poured into Tank C. After that, 4 full buckets of water are removed from Tank C. Each bucket has a volume of 1 ℓ. How much water, in liters and milliliters, is then left in Tank C?

End-Of-Year Review

Section A

Four options are given for each question. Only one of them is correct. Choose the correct answer and write its number in the parentheses.

1. 80 thousands, 8 hundreds and 8 ones written as a number is _____.
    (1) 8880   (2) 8808
    (3) 80,800   (4) 80,808   (   )

2. A 2-digit number gives a remainder of 5 when divided by 8. It gives a remainder of 2 when divided by 5. What is the number?
    (1) 37   (2) 45
    (3) 61   (4) 78   (   )

3. Which of the following is not a number pattern?
    (1) 36, 72, 144, 288   (2) 30, 26, 22, 18
    (3) 850, 865, 880, 890   (4) 14, 17, 20, 23   (   )

4. Roy's age this year is a multiple of 5. Next year his age will be a multiple of 7. What is Roy's present age?
    (1) 20   (2) 35
    (3) 70   (4) 90   (   )

5. $\frac{2}{3}$ of $42 is _____.
    (1) $14   (2) $28
    (3) $39   (4) $54   (   )

6. What fraction of 3 years is 8 months?

    (1) $\frac{1}{3}$ (2) $\frac{1}{4}$

    (3) $\frac{3}{8}$ (4) $\frac{2}{9}$ (   )

7. Which of the following sets of fractions is arranged in descending order?

(1) $\dfrac{1}{8}, \dfrac{3}{10}, \dfrac{1}{2}, \dfrac{4}{5}$

(2) $\dfrac{4}{5}, \dfrac{1}{2}, \dfrac{3}{10}, \dfrac{1}{8}$

(3) $\dfrac{4}{5}, \dfrac{3}{10}, \dfrac{1}{8}, \dfrac{1}{2}$

(4) $\dfrac{1}{2}, \dfrac{1}{8}, \dfrac{4}{5}, \dfrac{3}{10}$

( )

8. Which one of the following is not equivalent to $\dfrac{9}{10}$?

(1) $\dfrac{45}{50}$

(2) $9 \div 10$

(3) 0.9

(4) $10 \div 9$

( )

9. Express 3.6 as a fraction in its lowest term.

(1) $3\dfrac{6}{50}$

(2) $3\dfrac{6}{100}$

(3) $3\dfrac{6}{10}$

(4) $3\dfrac{3}{5}$

( )

10. Mrs. Baker baked 3 cheese cakes. Her husband ate $\dfrac{1}{3}$ of all the cheese cakes. Her son ate $\dfrac{2}{3}$ of a cheese cake. How many cheese cakes did Mrs. Baker have left?

(1) 1

(2) 2

(3) $1\dfrac{1}{3}$

(4) $2\dfrac{1}{3}$

( )

11. Look at the diagram and answer the question that follows.

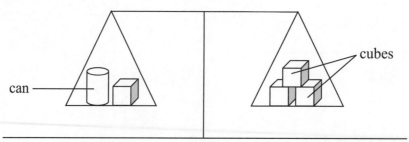

If each cube weighs $\dfrac{3}{5}$ g, how much does a can weigh?

(1) $\dfrac{2}{5}$ g

(2) $\dfrac{1}{5}$ g

(3) $1\dfrac{1}{5}$ g

(4) $2\dfrac{2}{5}$ g

( )

12.　　**R S T L N E**

Which letters are made up of perpendicular lines **only**?
(1)　T and L　　　　　　　　　(2)　N and E
(3)　T and E　　　　　　　　　(4)　R and N　　　　　　(　)

13.　The value of the digit '4' in 2.943 is _____.
(1)　4　　　　　　　　　　　　(2)　0.4
(3)　0.04　　　　　　　　　　　(4)　0.004　　　　　　(　)

14.　The value of 72.95 when rounded to 1 decimal place is _____.
(1)　72.9　　　　　　　　　　　(2)　7.29
(3)　73　　　　　　　　　　　　(4)　73.0　　　　　　(　)

15.　Express the sum of 3, $\frac{3}{10}$ and $\frac{6}{50}$ as a decimal.

(1)　3.42　　　　　　　　　　　(2)　3.36
(3)　3.312　　　　　　　　　　　(4)　3.18　　　　　　(　)

16.　The graph shows the time taken by 4 runners in a 100-meter race.

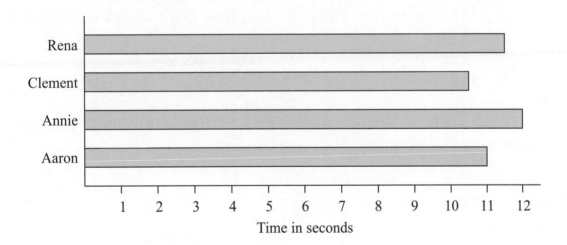

Who came in second in the race?
(1)　Rena　　　　　　　　　　　(2)　Clement
(3)　Annie　　　　　　　　　　　(4)　Aaron　　　　　　(　)

17. Which of these figures has the smallest perimeter?

(1)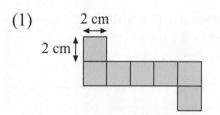

(2)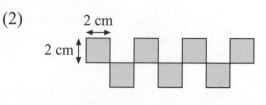

(3)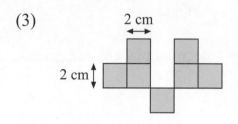

(4)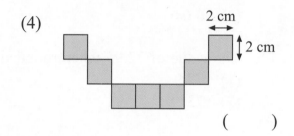

( )

18. A square of sides 6.5 cm has the same perimeter as a rectangle whose width is 3 cm. What is the area of the rectangle?
    (1) 9.5 cm^2 (2) 19.5 cm^2
    (3) 26 cm^2 (4) 30 cm^2 ( )

19. Sulaiman bought 7 mangoes at 75 cents each and 6 pears at 45 cents each. He paid the stallholder with a $10-bill. How much change did Sulaiman receive?
    (1) $2.05   (2) $3.05
    (3) $3.92   (4) $7.95   ( )

20. Which circle(s), when removed from the figure, will make the figure symmetrical?

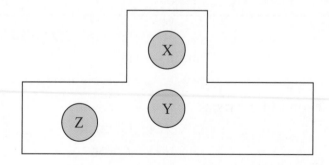

    (1) X   (2) Y
    (3) Z   (4) X and Y   ( )

Section B

Write your answers in the spaces provided.
Answers must be in the units stated.

21. $489 \times 39 = (400 \times 39) + (\boxed{} \times 39)$

The missing number in the box is _____.

_____

22. A number when rounded off to the nearest ten is 750. It is 800 when rounded to the nearest hundred. What is this number if it is also a multiple of 4?

_____

23. $\dfrac{13}{4} + \boxed{}$ is smaller than 9.

What is the largest whole number that you can put in the box to make the statement true?

_____

24. 18,081 m can be written as _____ km _____ m.

_____ km _____ m

25. Arrange the following measurements in order, beginning with the smallest. Include the units in your answer.

$$3.2 \text{ ft, } 3\frac{1}{2} \text{ ft, } 20 \text{ in, } 1\frac{1}{2} \text{ yd}$$

_____

26. Find the perimeter of the figure. (All lines meet at right angles.)

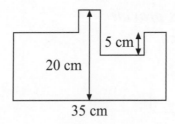

_____ cm

27. What is the area of the figure? (All lines meet at right angles.)

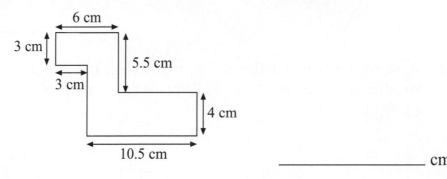

_____ cm²

28. A straight line passes through a rectangle as shown. Find ∠x.

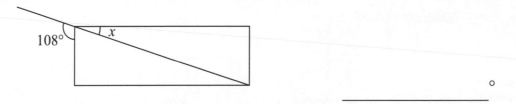

_____ °

29. Name a pair of parallel lines from the set of lines.

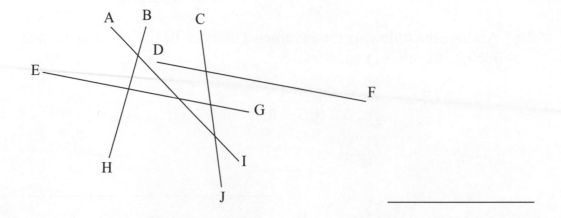

_____

30. Melissa had twice as much money as Reggie. After Melissa had spent $200, Reggie then had $25 more than Melissa. How much money did Melissa have at first?

$ _____

31. An empty bowl weighs 750 g. After some beans are put into it, the bowl of beans weighs 1 kg 60 g. How much do the beans weigh?

_____ g

32.

> Shirley weighs 77.2 lb
> Kim weighs 90.4 lb
> Sharon weighs 120.2 lb

How much do the three girls weigh altogether?

_____ lb

33. Alice works from 8:30 am to 5:30 pm on weekdays and from 9:00 am to 1:00 pm on Saturdays. How many hours does she work in a week?

_____ h

34. Shirley is now 11 yr 9 mth old. Her classmate is $\frac{1}{2}$ yr older than her. What is the total age of the two girls?

_____ years

35. The figure shows half of a symmetric figure.
Complete the figure with the dotted line as its line of symmetry.

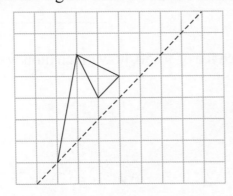

36. A bucket can hold 5 qt 3 c How many quarts and cups of water can 5 such buckets hold?

_____ qt _____ c

The graph shows the number of people who visited a trade fair in a week. Study it carefully and answer Questions 37 and 38.

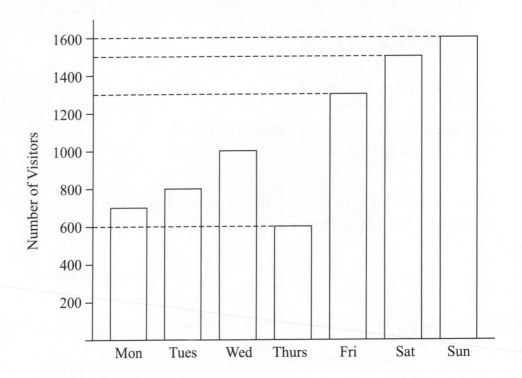

37. How many more people visited the trade fair on Sunday than on Thursday?

_____ people

38. If each visitor paid an entrance fee of $3.50, how much money was collected over the weekend?

$ _____

39. What fraction of the figure is unshaded? Give the answer as a decimal.

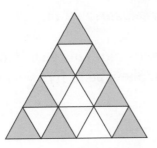

_____

40. How many unit cube(s) need to be removed from Figure A to form Figure B?

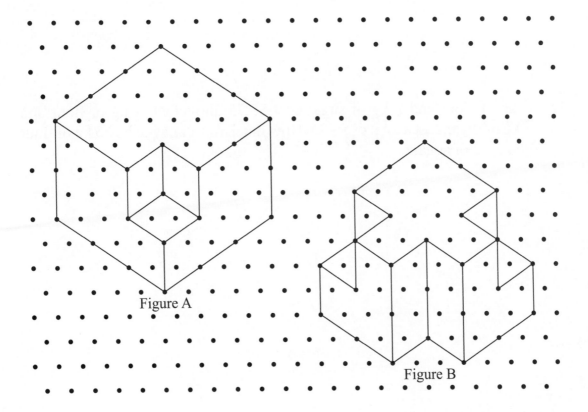

Figure A

Figure B

_____ cubes

Section C

For each question, show your work clearly in the space provided.

41. Five years ago, Pedro was 31 years old. This year Pedro is 4 times as old as his nephew. How old will his nephew be in five years' time?

42. 4 kg of flour and 1 kg of sugar cost $5.75 altogether. 2 kg of flour and 1 kg of sugar cost a total of $3.25. How much must I pay to buy 5 kg of flour and 5 kg of sugar?

43. Three sisters inherited $35,000.
Louisa received twice as much money as Joan while Audrey received half as much money as Joan. How much money did Joan receive?

44. Mrs. Cheery baked some cupcakes. She gave $\frac{1}{9}$ of the cupcakes to her neighbor. Her husband and children ate 28 cupcakes altogether. Mrs. Cheery still had $\frac{2}{3}$ of the cupcakes left.
    (a)   How many cupcakes did she bake?
    (b)   She sold the remaining cupcakes for $0.45 each. How much money did she collect from the sale?

45. The floor of a rectangular room 6 m wide, is to be laid with ceramic tiles. Two pieces of carpet 4 m by 4 m are to be placed on top of the tile as shown.

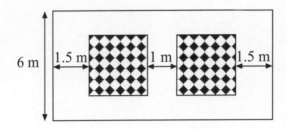

(a) If 12 identical ceramic tiles are required to be laid on each square meter of the floor, how many tiles are needed for the entire floor?

(b) What fraction of the floor is not covered by the two pieces of carpet?

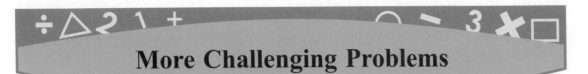

More Challenging Problems

1. Samuel wrote a composition at home on a Sunday morning. He looked at the reflection of the clock in the mirror in front of him at the start and at the end of his work.

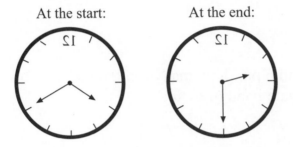

At the start: At the end:

   How long did Samuel take to write the composition?

2. Victor realizes that the time shown on his digital watch is 30 seconds faster than the time shown on his digital clock at home. However, the time shown on his digital clock is 30 seconds slower than the actual time. Is Victor's digital watch showing the actual time? If not, by how much is it faster or slower than the actual time?

3. A scientist carried out a very tedious experiment. He took a reading every 5 hours. At the 12th reading, the hour hand was pointing to the number 9. What number did the hour hand point to at the 2nd reading?

4. Between 2 pm and 6 pm, how many right angles are formed by the hour hand and the minute hand of a clock?

5. Four cats take 3 minutes to eat 4 fish altogether at the same time. With this same rate, how long will it take 120 cats to eat 120 fish altogether at the same time?

6. Kelvin can cut a piece of log into five pieces in 20 minutes. At the same rate, how long will Kelvin take to cut the log into eight pieces?

7. A clock takes 12 seconds to ring 3 times at 3 pm. How long does the clock take
    (a) to ring 6 times at 6 pm,
    (b) to ring 11 times at 11 pm?

8. The perimeter of a circular pond is 800 m. Small red light bulbs are fixed on the upper edge of the wall of the pond at 4 m apart. At the center of each pair of adjacent red light bulbs, there is a yellow light bulb. How many red and yellow light bulbs are there around the pond?

9. (a) There were 25 people at a birthday party. Each person shook hands exactly once with each of the others. How many handshakes were exchanged at the party?

(b) A number of tennis clubs are taking part in a competition. Every team in the competition has to play every other team just once. How many games will there be altogether if 80 teams take part in the competition?

10. You have exactly $4.40 in quarters, dimes, and nickels. How many of each coin do you have if you have the exact same number of each type of coin?

11. A man bought a greeting card at a shop for $4. He paid the cashier with a $10 bill. As the cashier did not have any small change, she went to the cashier next to her to exchange the $10 bill for smaller bills. She then gave the man his $6 change. Later on, the shopkeeper realized that the $10 bill was a counterfeit. How much did the shopkeeper lose altogether?

12. Mrs. Lim went to a bank to withdraw some money. She withdrew half of her savings and another $200. She then realized that she needed more cash, so she withdrew half of the remaining money less $50. She was then left with $950 after the second withdrawal. How much did she have at first?

13. In a social club, 38 people like to swim, 39 people like to play tennis and 5 people like neither. If there are 57 people in the club, how many people like both sports?

14. Two squares of sides 9 cm and 7 cm overlap as shown. Find the difference in the areas between the two shaded parts.

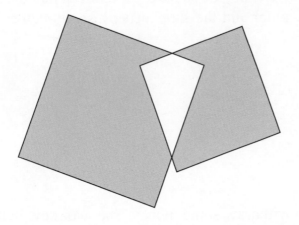

15. The big square consists of four identical rectangles and a small square. If the area of the big square is 49 cm² and the area of the small square is 4 cm², find the length and width of each rectangle.

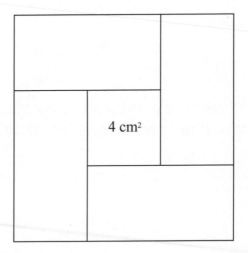

16. (a) The figure shows two equilateral triangles and a circle. If the area of the small equilateral triangle is 6 cm², what is the area of the big equilateral triangle?

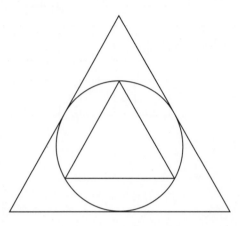

(b) The figure shows three equilateral triangles and two circles. If the area of the smallest equilateral triangle is 7 cm², what is the area of the biggest equilateral triangle?

17. In each of the following, fill in the boxes with different single-digit numbers to make the number sentences true.

(a)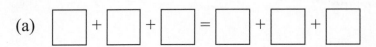

(b)

(c) $\square + \square - \square = \square \times \square \div \square$

18. In the following addition, A, B and C represent three different single-digit numbers. Among them, A is the largest number and C is the smallest. What numbers do A, B and C represent?

$$
\begin{array}{ccc}
 & A & B & C \\
 & B & C & A \\
+ & C & A & B \\
\hline
 & 7 & 7 & 7 \\
\hline
\end{array}
$$

Answers

Topic 1: Decimals

1.

Dollar bill	Number of $1 bills	Fraction of a $1000-bill		
		Decimal Fraction	Fraction	Decimal
One hundred	100	$\frac{100}{1000}$ or $\frac{10}{100}$	$\frac{1}{10}$	0.1
Fifty	50	$\frac{50}{1000}$ or $\frac{5}{100}$	$\frac{1}{20}$	0.05
Ten	10	$\frac{10}{1000}$	$\frac{1}{100}$	0.01
Five	5	$\frac{5}{1000}$	$\frac{1}{200}$	0.005
One	1	$\frac{1}{1000}$	$\frac{1}{1000}$	0.001

2. (a) 123.45   (b) 707.07
   (c) 6380.083   (d) 82.304
   (e) 7045.009

3. (a) $\frac{1}{10} = 0.1$ (b) $\frac{5}{10} = 0.5$
   (c) $\frac{4}{10} = 0.4$ (d) $\frac{7}{10} = 0.7$
   (e) $\frac{3}{5} = \frac{6}{10} = 0.6$

4. (a) 0.2   (b) 0.8
   (c) 1   (d) 1.6
   (e) 2.6   (f) 16.9

5. (a) 500   (b) 1
   (c) 100   (d) 34
   (e) 126   (f) 75

6. (a) 3   (b) tenths
   (c) 0.9   (d) 40
   (e) 15   (f) 26.8
   (g) 4   (h) 12

7. (a) 0.9   (b) 0.3
   (c) 1.4   (d) 4.2
   (e) 8.5   (f) 10.6

8. (a) 1.3   (b) 0.3
   (c) 0.9   (d) 8.8

9. (a) $\frac{7}{10}$ (b) $1\frac{1}{5}$
   (c) $4\frac{2}{5}$ (d) $7\frac{4}{5}$
   (e) $13\frac{3}{5}$ (f) $20\frac{9}{10}$

10. (a) 2.9   (b) 0.8
    (c) 5.5   (d) 5.3
    (e) 12.8   (f) 13.7

11. (a) 0.3, 1.7, 2.5, 3.9
    (b) 0.1, 6.6, 7.3, 8.4, 9.8
    (c) 0.2, 11.4, 13.8, 15.2, 16.6
    (d) 0.2, 49.8, 51.2, 53.4, 54.8

12. (a)   (b)

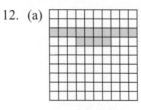 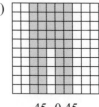

14, 0.14   45, 0.45

(c)

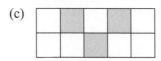

30, 30, 0.30

(d)

40, 40, 0.40

(e)

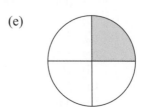

25, 25, 0.25

(f)

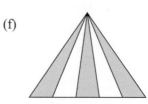

60, 60, 0.60

13. (a) 0.02   (b) 0.18
    (c) 1   (d) 4.93
    (e) 0.37   (f) 1.73

14. (a) 32.46   (b) 103.96
    (c) 72.22   (d) 610.93

15. (a) 8   (b) 80
    (c) 8   (d) 88
    (e) 180   (f) 180

16. (a) hundredths   (b) 3
    (c) 400   (d) 0.05
    (e) 100   (f) 0.17

17. (a) 0.09   (b) 0.75
    (c) 1.25   (d) 4.16
    (e) 7.85   (f) 10.44

18. (a) $\frac{2}{25}$ (b) $\frac{23}{100}$

    (c) $\frac{3}{5}$ (d) $1\frac{43}{50}$

    (e) $3\frac{3}{4}$ (f) $26\frac{1}{20}$

19. (a) 6.06   (b) 18.19
    (c) 9.04   (d) 20.1
    (e) 100.2   (f) 103.7

20. (a) 0.36, 0.47, 0.53, 0.69
    (b) 0.01, 6.27, 6.41, 6.53, 6.61
    (c) 0.02, 9.22, 9.38, 9.56, 9.72
    (d) 0.02, 1.0, 1.32, 1.46, 1.58

21. (a) $\frac{6}{100}$ (b) $\frac{5}{100}$

    (c) $\frac{7}{10}$ (d) $\frac{11}{10}$

22. (a) 8.17   (b) 12.05
    (c) 17.66   (d) 91.6

23. (a) 0.005   (b) 0.375
    (c) 0.040   (d) 0.108
    (e) 1.234   (f) 3.145

24. (a) 0.255   (b) 1.521
    (c) 12.052   (d) 40.119

25. (a) thousandths   (b) 6
    (c) 4000   (d) 0.007
    (e) 100   (f) 1.997

26. (a) 0.106   (b) 0.080
    (c) 1.045   (d) 5.950
    (e) 29.416   (f) 14.125

27. (a) $\frac{3}{500}$ (b) $\frac{3}{40}$

    (c) $\frac{111}{200}$ (d) $1\frac{1}{50}$

    (e) $7\frac{3}{8}$ (f) $2\frac{12}{25}$

28. (a) 0.023, 0.203, 0.302, 2.003
    (b) 1.083, 1.38, 3.018, 3.108

    (c) 1.005, $\frac{21}{20}$, $2\frac{1}{5}$, 2.5

    (d) $3\frac{106}{1000}$, $3\frac{6}{10}$, $4\frac{7}{8}$, 4.951

29. (a) 8.382, 3.8, 2.083, 0.832
    (b) 89.09, 10.809, 9.908, 9.089

    (c) $\frac{23}{10}$, 1.555, $1\frac{1}{2}$, 0.742

    (d) 20.19, $2\frac{19}{100}$, 2.109, $1\frac{9}{10}$

30. (a) 1.006, 1.017, 1.023, 1.039
    (b) 0.001, 10.077, 10.084, 10.10, 10.113
    (c) 0.002, 4.018, 4.034, 4.052, 4.066
    (d) 0.002, 8.135, 8.151, 8.167, 8.183

31. (a) $\frac{8}{100}$ (b) $\frac{59}{1000}$

    (c) $\frac{9}{1000}$ (d) $\frac{19}{10}$

32. (a) 3.67   (b) 10.45
    (c) 15.286   (d) 81.561

33. (a) 5   (b) 0
    (c) 10   (d) 38
    (e) 3   (f) 15

34. (a) 0.9   (b) 4.6
    (c) 10.4   (d) 27.1
    (e) 6.8   (f) 0.3
    (g) 56.7   (h) 23.0

35. (a) 0.26   (b) 0.57
    (c) 1.08   (d) 34.70
    (e) 29.27   (f) 99.90
    (g) 1.00   (h) 2.00

36. (a) 3.5, 3.6, 3.7, 3.8, 3.9, 4.0, 4.1, 4.2, 4.3, 4.4
    (b) 9.5, 9.6, 9.7, 9.8, 9.9, 10.0, 10.1, 10.2, 10.3, 10.4
    (c) 124.5, 124.6, 124.7, 124.8, 124.9, 125.0, 125.1, 125.2, 125.3, 125.4

37. (a) 0.85, 0.86, 0.87, 0.88, 0.89, 0.90, 0.91, 0.92, 0.93, 0.94
    (b) 13.75, 13.76, 13.77, ..., 13.82, 13.83, 13.84
    (c) 199.95, 199.96, 199.97, ..., 200.03, 200.04

38. (a) 0.565, 0.566, 0.567, ..., 0.572, 0.573, 0.574
    (b) 8.345, 8.346, 8.347, ..., 8.352, 8.353, 8.354
    (c) 12.195, 12.196, ..., 12.200, 12.201, 12.202, 12.203, 12.204

39. (a) 71 lb   (b) 20 yd
    (c) $25   (d) 300 km

40. (a) $10.45, $10.52, $10.49
    (b) 78.04 m, 77.95 m, 77.973 m
    (c) 24.95 gal, 24.75 gal, 25.045 gal

Topic 2: The Four Operations of Decimals

1. (a) 0.83   (b) 0.17
  (c) 1.35   (d) 1.16
  (e) 7.03   (f) 1.43
  (g) 1.9   (h) 1.27
2. (a) 1.39   (b) 1.62
  (c) 6.89   (d) 3.16
  (e) 13.33   (f) 5.07
  (g) 22.96   (h) 59.63
  (i) 32.42   (j) 71.34
3. (a) 11   (b) $3 + 9 = 12$
  (c) $5 + 2 = 7$ (d) $10 + 4 = 14$
  (e) $27 + 1 = 28$ (f) $13 + 48 = 61$
4. (a) 0.04   (b) 0.61
  (c) 1.21   (d) 0.94
  (e) 3.97   (f) 2.53
  (g) 13.36   (h) 16.89
  (i) 32.68   (j) 4.46
5. (a) 5   (b) $9 - 3 = 6$
  (c) $11 - 5 = 6$ (d) $5 - 1 = 4$
  (e) $26 - 15 = 11$ (f) $17 - 9 = 8$
6. (a) 6, 0.03, 21.77   (b) 11, 0.01, 32.67
  (c) 3.14   (d) 7, 0.04, 3.73
  (e) 14, 0.01, 18.54

7. (a)

0.7	0.8	0.3
0.2	0.6	1
0.9	0.4	0.5

(b)

1.5	1.25	2.5
2.75	1.75	0.75
1	2.25	2

(c)

0.65	0.15	0.85
0.75	0.55	0.35
0.25	0.95	0.45

(d)

1.3	0.7	0.7
0.3	0.9	1.5
1.1	1.1	0.5

8. (a) 2.78   (b) 9.61
  (c) 171.8   (d) 10.36
  (e) 10.08   (f) $74.70
  (g) 8.75 m   (h) 3.31 qt
  (i) 9.98 s   (j) 0.55 h
9. (a) 0.12   (b) 3.6
  (c) 5.4   (d) 0.48
  (e) 0.39   (f) 24.36
  (g) 3.40   (h) 16.12
  (i) 67.44   (j) 348.75
  (k) 925.2   (l) 734.3

10. (a) 42   (b) $15 \times 7 = 105$
  (c) $17 \times 3 = 51$ (d) $5 \times 34 = 170$
  (e) $42 \times 9 = \$378$ (f) $3 \times 85 = \$255$
11. (a) 0.3   (b) 0.07
  (c) 0.9   (d) 0.8
  (e) 0.35   (f) 0.46

```
      0.3 5              0.4 6
  2)0.7 0            5)2.3 0
   - 0                - 0
     7                  2 3
   - 6                - 2 0
     1 0                  3 0
   - 1 0                - 3 0
       0                    0
```

  (g) 0.25   (h) 3.75
  (i) 2.53   (j) 3.51
  (k) 13.04   (l) 13.19
12. (a) 28, 27.9   (b) 25, 25.3
  (c) 1, 0.9   (d) 8, 8.3
  (e) 4, 3.5   (f) 12, 11.5
  (g) 3, 3.1   (h) 4, 3.8
  (i) 95, 94.7   (j) 58, 57.8
  (k) 13, 13.0   (l) 275, 274.5
13. (a) 0.60   (b) 3.14
  (c) 1.84   (d) 5.98
14. (a) 2   (b) 0.2
  (c) $28 \div 7 = 4$ (d) $32 \div 8 = 4$
  (e) $72 \div 9 = 8$ (f) $236 \div 4 = 59$
15. (a) 2.4, 2.8   (b) 4.25, 3.25
  (c) 2, 4.5   (d) 6.4, 0.1
  (e) 1311   (f) 1.85 kg
  (g) 4.725 m
  (h) Area = 160.2 cm^2
     Perimeter = 53.6 cm
  (i) 22 ℓ
  (j) $4.30
  (k) 1.67 ft

Word Problems

1. $9.65   2. 21.7 gal
3. 72 km   4. 3 rolls
5. $145.20   6. 3.5 kg
7. 9.34 kg   8. $560
9. 97.36 kg   10. $4
11. $18.60
12. (a) $20.85   (b) $45.15 more
13. Orange → $0.50
    Mango → $2
14. 40 students   15. 23 stamps

Take the Challenge!

1. $\dfrac{111}{500} = \dfrac{100}{500} + \dfrac{10}{500} + \dfrac{1}{500}$

   $= \dfrac{1}{5} + \dfrac{1}{50} + \dfrac{1}{500}$

   $= 0.2 + 0.02 + 0.002$

   $= 0.222$

2. Difference in cost of peanuts must be equal to the difference in cost of cashew nuts.
   Increase in cost of peanuts
   $= 12 \times (8.40 - 6) = \$28.80$
   Price of cashew nuts reduced by
   $\$12 - \$8.40 = \$3.60$
   Cashew nuts $\rightarrow 28.80 \div 3.60 = 8$ kg

3. If all the 40 problems were correct, she would score
   $\rightarrow 2.5 \times 40 = 100$
   Difference $= 100 - 75.5 = 24.5$
   For every wrong answer, she lost
   $2.5 + 1 = 3.5$
   $24.5 \div 3.5 = 7$ wrong answers
   $40 - 7 = 33$ correct answers

Topic 3: Measures

1. (a) 384   (b) 3
   (c) 7, 3   (d) 1273
   (e) 5000   (f) 4, 70
   (g) 6575   (h) 7
   (i) 9, 304   (j) 5, 26
   (k) 2   (l) 6493
   (m) 9, 4   (n) 45
   (o) 100   (p) 5, 2
   (q) 144   (r) 2, 1
2. (a) 180   (b) 85
   (c) 4   (d) 2, 18
   (e) 2   (f) 3, 23
   (g) 480   (h) 159
3. (a) 21 m 78 cm   (b) 28 km 332 m
   (c) 18 h 35 min   (d) 84 min 56 s
   (e) 51 ft   (f) 61 gal 1 qt
4. (a) 1 m 56 cm   (b) 5 km 813 m
   (c) 2 kg 18 g   (d) 1 ℓ 133 ml
   (e) 4 h 11 min   (f) 1 ft 9 in.
5. (a) 4.85   (b) 15.264
   (c) 3.455   (d) 1.890
   (e) 145.65   (f) 11.035

Word Problems

1. 11 ℓ 340 ml   2. 1 kg 78 g
3. $15.50   4. 1 m 38 cm

5. (a) 57 h   (b) $342
6. $47.60
7. (a) 1 kg 84 g   (b) 22 kg 764 g
8. (a) 17 yd   (b) $178.50
9. 5 kg 530 g   10. 96 ℓ 30 ml

Topic 4: Symmetry

1. (a) ✓   (b) ✗   (c) ✓
   (d) ✓   (e) ✗   (f) ✗
   (g) ✗   (h) ✓

2.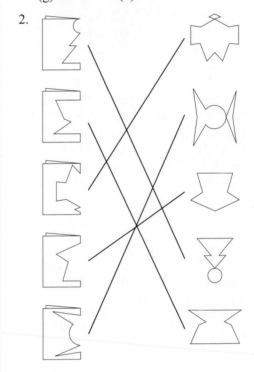

3. (a)

   (b)

   (c)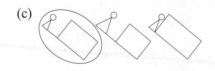

   (d)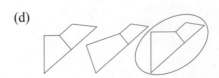

4. (a) ✓   (b) ✗   (c) ✓
   (d) ✓   (e) ✗   (f) ✗

5. (a)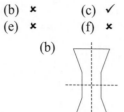

   (b)

   (c)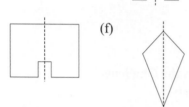

   (d)

   (e)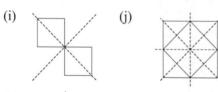

   (f)

   (g)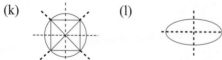

   (h)

   (i)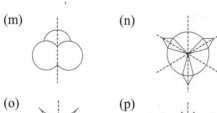

   (j)

   (k)

   (l)

   (m)

   (n)

   (o)

   (p)

6. (a)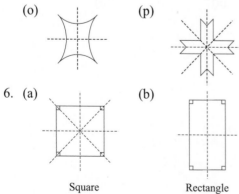

   Square

   (b)

   Rectangle

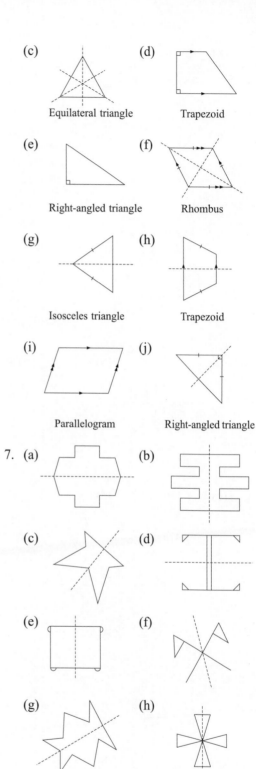

(c)

   Equilateral triangle

(d)

   Trapezoid

(e)

   Right-angled triangle

(f)

   Rhombus

(g)

   Isosceles triangle

(h)

   Trapezoid

(i)

   Parallelogram

(j)

   Right-angled triangle

7. (a)   (b)

   (c)   (d)

   (e)   (f)

   (g)   (h)

   (i)   (j)

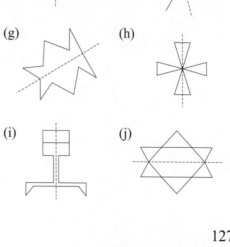

(k)  (l)

(i) 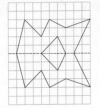 (j)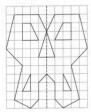

(m) (n)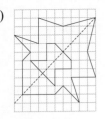

(o) 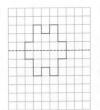 (p)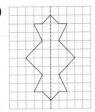

(k)

(l)

Take the Challenge!

1. (a) (b)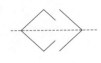

8. (a) (b)

(c) (d)

(c) 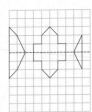 (d)

(e) (f)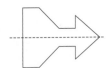

(e) 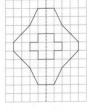 (f)

(g) (h)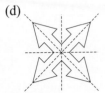

(g) 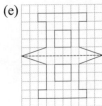 (h)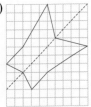

2. (a)  (b)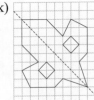

(c) (d)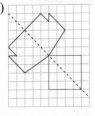

128

3.

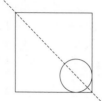

4. (a)

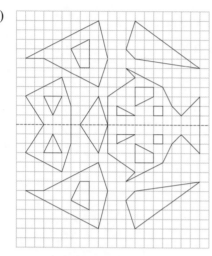

(b)

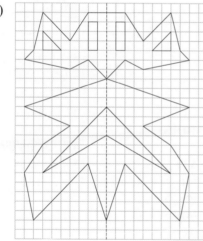

Topic 5: Solid Figures

1. (a) 24   (b) 6
   (c) 6   (d) 12
   (e) 44   (f) 16
   (g) 20   (h) 19
   (i) 18   (j) 11
2. (a) 17   (b) 11
   (c) 9   (d) 15
   (e) 20   (f) 18
   (g) 52   (h) 19
   (i) 56   (j) 33

3. (a) 20   (b) 24
   (c) 12   (d) 39
   (e) 30   (f) 9
   (g) 21   (h) 33
   (i) 28   (j) 33
4. (a) 2   (b) 2
   (c) 3   (d) 3
   (e) 3   (f) 3
   (g) 4   (h) 5
5. (a) 5   (b) 2
   (c) 3   (d) 3
   (e) 4   (f) 2
   (g) 3   (h) 4
6. (a) Circle (iii)   (b) Circle (iv)
   (c) Circle (ii)

Take the Challenge!

1. (a) 3   (b) 4
   (c) 4   (d) 4
2. (a) 6   (b) 4
   (c) 8   (d) 3

Topic 6: Volume

1. (a) 5   (b) 16
   (c) 14   (d) 7
   (e) 6   (f) 7
   (g) 10   (h) 14
   (i) 8   (j) 7
   (k) 12   (l) 11
2. (a) 10   (b) 7
   (c) 6   (d) 11
   (e) 16   (f) 36
   (g) 9   (h) 16
   (i) 12   (j) 16
   (k) 19   (l) 48
3. (a) 4 cm, 1 cm, 1 cm, 4 cm^3
   (b) 1 cm, 1 cm, 4 cm, 4 cm^3
   (c) 3 cm, 2 cm, 1 cm, 6 cm^3
   (d) 2 cm, 2 cm, 6 cm, 24 cm^3
   (e) 4 cm, 3 cm, 2 cm, 24 cm^3
   (f) 6 cm, 2 cm, 5 cm, 60 cm^3
   (g) 4 cm, 3 cm, 5 cm, 60 cm^3
   (h) 6 cm, 5 cm, 3 cm, 90 cm^3
4. (a) 105 cm^3 (b) 180 cm^3
   (c) 24 m^3 (d) 60 m^3
   (e) 56 in.^{3} (f) 156 ft^3
5. (a) 1000 cm^3 (b) 562 cm^3
   (c) 38,000 cm^3 (d) 73 cm^3
   (e) 6520 cm^3 (f) $\frac{1}{2}$ cm^3

(g) 15,005 cm³ (h) 3060 cm³
(i) 800 cm³ (j) 300 cm³

6. (a) 19 ml (b) 275 ml
   (c) 1 ℓ 598 ml (d) 8 ℓ 95 ml
   (e) 36 ℓ 427 ml (f) 0.72 ml
   (g) 206 ℓ 381 ml (h) 10 ℓ 58 ml
   (i) 1 ℓ 0.2 ml (j) 38.5 ml

7. (a) 280 ml (b) 40 ml
   (c) 560 ml (d) 450 ml
   (e) 120 ml (f) 660 ml
   (g) 320 ml (h) 390 ml
   (i) 150 ml (j) 504 ml
   (k) 360 ml (l) 72 ml

8. (a) 3 ℓ (b) 7 ℓ
   (c) 16 ℓ (d) 9 ℓ
   (e) 12 ℓ (f) 6 ℓ
   (g) 3 ℓ (h) 9 ℓ
   (i) 6 ℓ (j) 60 ℓ
   (k) 17 ℓ (l) 13 ℓ

9. (a) 2 ℓ 128 ml (b) 6 ℓ 720 ml
   (c) 4 ℓ 862 ml (d) 1 ℓ 320 ml
   (e) 5 ℓ 550 ml (f) 3 ℓ 600 ml
   (g) 2 ℓ 200 ml (h) 2 ℓ 800 ml
   (i) 8 ℓ 320 ml (j) 4 ℓ 752 ml
   (k) 29 ℓ 120 ml (l) 9 ℓ 576 ml

Word Problems

1. 750 cm³ 2. 3600 m³
3. 80 ℓ 4. 8 ℓ 750 ml
5. 23 ℓ 500 ml 6. 3 ℓ
7. 3000 ml 8. 260 ml
9. 0.3 ℓ 10. 1500 cm³

Take the Challenge!

1. Volume of 1 cube = 3 × 3 × 3 = 27 cm³
   Volume of 6 cubes = 27 × 6 = 162 cm³
   ∴ Volume of water = 162 cm³ = 162 ml

2. Volume of water in Tank A
   = 12 × 6 × 5 = 360 cm³
   Volume of water in Tank B
   = 8 × 5 × 9 = 360 cm³
   Volume of water in Tank C
   = 30 × 15 × 10 = 4500 cm³
   Total volume of water in Tank C
   = 360 + 360 + 4500 = 5220 cm³
   Volume of 4 buckets = 4 × 1
   = 4 × 1000 cm³ = 4000 cm³
   ∴ Volume of water left = 5220 – 4000
   = 1220 cm³ = 1 ℓ 220 ml

End-Of-Year Review

1. 4 2. 1 3. 3 4. 1
5. 2 6. 4 7. 2 8. 4
9. 4 10. 3 11. 3 12. 1
13. 3 14. 4 15. 1 16. 4
17. 1 18. 4 19. 1 20. 3
21. 89 22. 752 23. 5 24. 18, 81

25. 20 in, 3.2 ft, $3\frac{1}{2}$ ft, $1\frac{1}{2}$ yd

26. 120 27. 67.5
28. 18 29. DF // EG
30. 350 31. 310
32. 287.8 33. 49
34. 24

35.

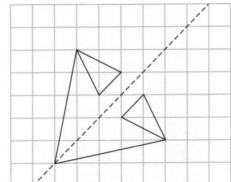

36. 28, 3 37. 1000
38. 10,850 39. 0.5
40. 3 41. 14 yrs old
42. $10 43. $10,000
44. (a) 126 cupcakes
    (b) $37.80
45. (a) 864 tiles
    (b) $\frac{5}{9}$

More Challenging Problems

1. Samuel started his work at 8:20 am and ended at 9:30 am.
   He took 1 hour and 10 minutes to complete his work.

2. The actual time is 30 seconds faster than the time shown on the digital clock.
   Since Victor's digital watch is 30 seconds faster than the time shown on his digital clock, his digital watch is showing the correct time.

3.

No. of reading	Number which hour hand was pointing to
12	9
11	4
10	11
9	6
8	1
7	8
6	3
5	10
4	5
3	12
2	7

The hour hand pointed to 7.

4. 7 right angles are formed.

5. 1 cat takes 3 minutes to eat 1 fish.
120 cats will also take 3 minutes to eat 120 fish altogether at the same time.

6. 4 cuts are needed to make 5 pieces.
So each cut takes 5 minutes.
To get 8 pieces, 7 cuts are needed.
$7 \times 5 = 35$ minutes
35 minutes are needed to cut 8 pieces.

7. At 3 pm:

Number of seconds = $(3 - 1) \times 6 = 12$
(a) Number of seconds = $(6 - 1) \times 6 = 30$
(b) Number of seconds = $(11 - 1)\ 6 = 60$

8. $800 \div 4 = 200$
There are 200 red light bulbs and 200 yellow light bulbs.

9. (a) Number of handshakes = $(25 \times 24) \div 2$
$= 300$
(b) Number of games $= (80 \times 78) \div 2$
$= 3120$

10. 11 of each. Divide 440 cents by $(25 + 10 + 5)$ to get 11, which means 11 of each coin.

11. The cashier lost $6 altogether.

12. *Method 1:*
Working backwards:
$[(950 - 50) \times 2 + 200] \times 2 = 4000$
She had $4000 at first.

Method 2:
Use models:

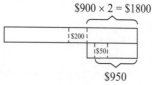

$2 \times (\$1800 + \$200) = \$4000$
She had $4000 at first.

13.

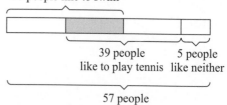

Number of people who like both sports
$= (38 + 39) - (57 - 5)$
$= 25$

14. Difference in the areas between the two shaded parts
= Area of big square – area of small square
$= (9 \times 9) - (7 \times 7)$
$= 81 - 49$
$= 32$ cm^2

15. Length of side of small square = 2 cm
Length of side of big square = 7 cm
$2 \times$ width of rectangle + length of side of small square = length of side of big square
$2 \times$ width of rectangle = $7 - 2 = 5$ cm
Width of rectangle = 2.5 cm
Length of each rectangle
= width of rectangle + length of side of small square
$= 2.5 + 2$
$= 4.5$ cm

16. (a) The small equilateral triangle can be rotated round the circle as shown:

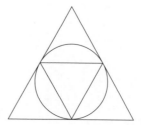

Hence the area of the small equilateral triangle is $\frac{1}{4}$ that of the big equilateral triangle.

Area of the big equilateral triangle
$= 4 \times 6 = 24$ cm^2

(b) Area of the second equilateral triangle
$= 4 \times 7 = 28$ cm^2

Area of the big equilateral triangle
$= 4 \times 28 = 112$ cm^2

17. Suggested solutions:
   (a) $7 + 5 + 2 = 9 + 4 + 1$
   (b) $(9 - 8) \times 6 = 4 \div 2 \times 3$
   (c) $5 + 9 - 8 = 4 \times 3 \div 2$

18. *Solution:*

```
    4 2 1
    2 1 4
+   1 4 2
---------
    7 7 7
---------
```

$A = 4$, $B = 2$, $C = 1$